E S T A T E   P U B L

SLOUGH·WINDSOR

COOKHAM · FARNHAM COMMON · OLI

C000111889

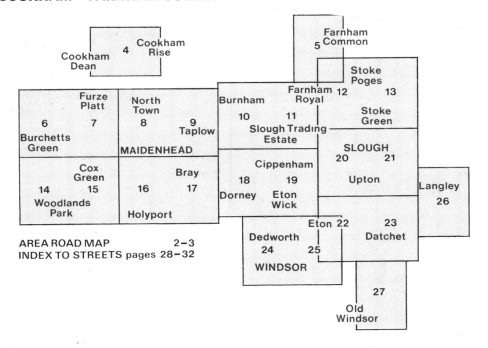

AREA ROAD MAP   2–3
INDEX TO STREETS pages 28–32

Legend	
One-way street	→
Pedestrianized	▨
Car Park	P
Post Office	●
Public Convenience	C
Place of worship	+
Scale of Street Plans 4 inches to 1 mile	

Street plans prepared and published by ESTATE PUBLICATIONS, Bridewell House, Tenterden, Kent. and based upon the ORDNANCE SURVEY maps with the sanction of the controller of H.M. Stationery Office.

The publishers acknowledge the co-operation of Slough Corporation Royal Borough of Windsor and Maidenhead and South Bucks District Council.

0 86084 605 9

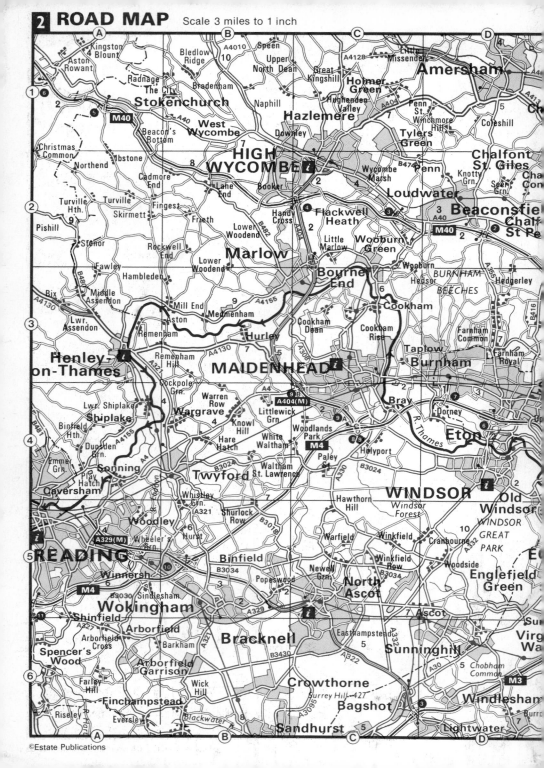

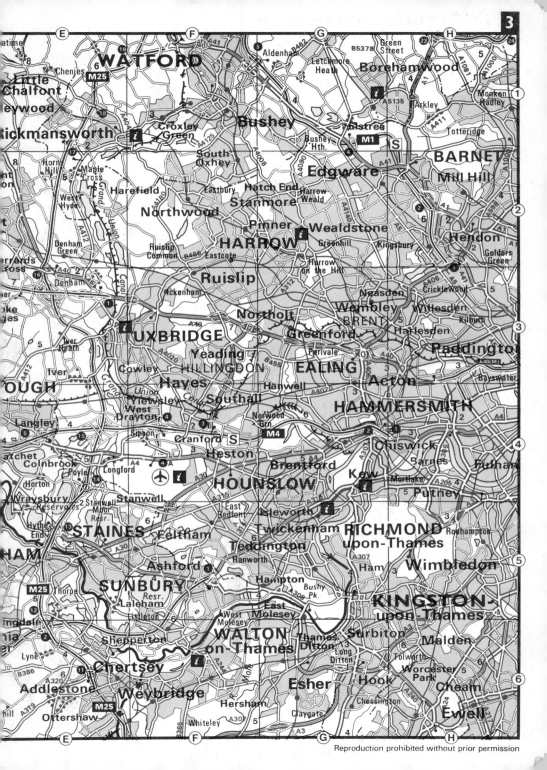

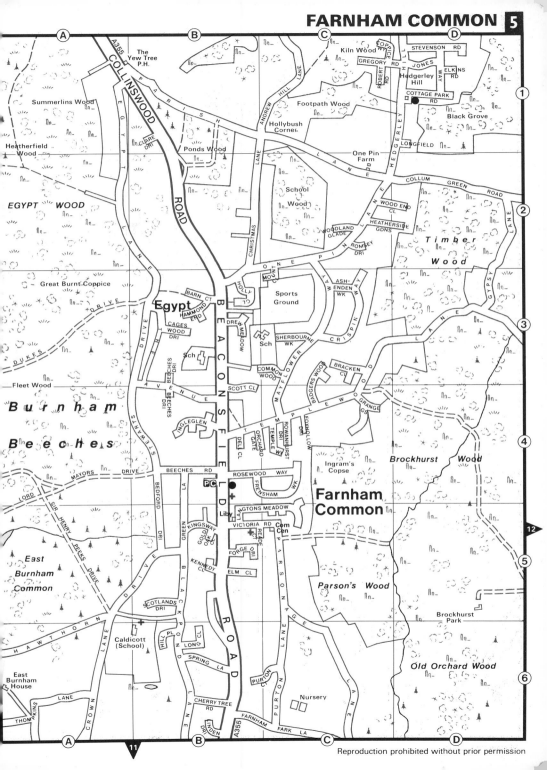

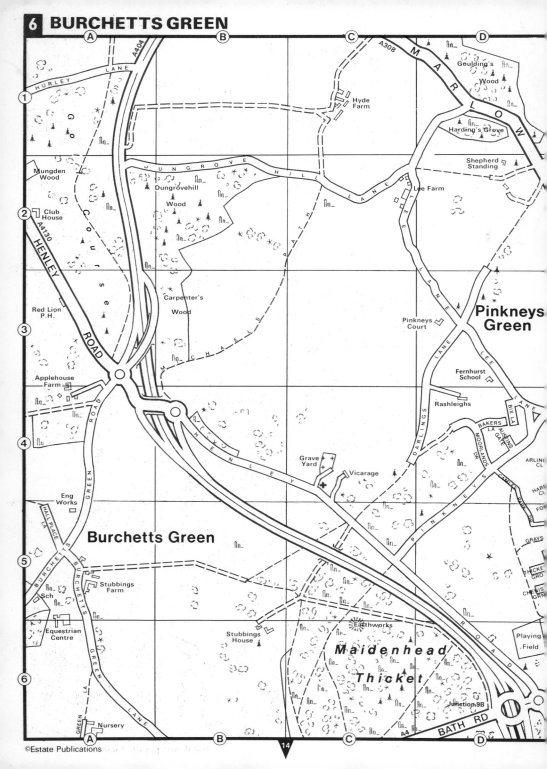

HURLEY LANE

A404

A308

MARLOW

Goulding's Wood

Hyde Farm

Harding's Grove

Shepherd Standing

GO

Mungden Wood

DUNGROVE HILL LANE

Dungrovehill Wood

Lee Farm

Club House

Course

A4130

HENLEY ROAD

Red Lion P.H.

Carpenter's Wood

ST MICHAELS PATH

Pinkneys Court

LEE LANE

Pinkneys Green

Fernhurst School

Applehouse Farm

HENLEY ROAD

Rashleighs

DARLINGS

MOORLANDS DR

BIX LA

BAKERS LA

AUSTINS GATE

ARLING CL

GREEN ROAD

Eng Works

Grave Yard

Vicarage

PINKNEYS ROAD

HARE CL

FO

HALL PLACE LA

BURCHETTS GREEN LA

Burchetts Green

GRAYS

THICKE GRO

CHENIS GR

Sch

Stubbings Farm

Equestrian Centre

Stubbings House

Earthworks

Maidenhead Thicket

Playing Field

GREEN LANE

Nursery

Junction 9B

BATH RD

A4

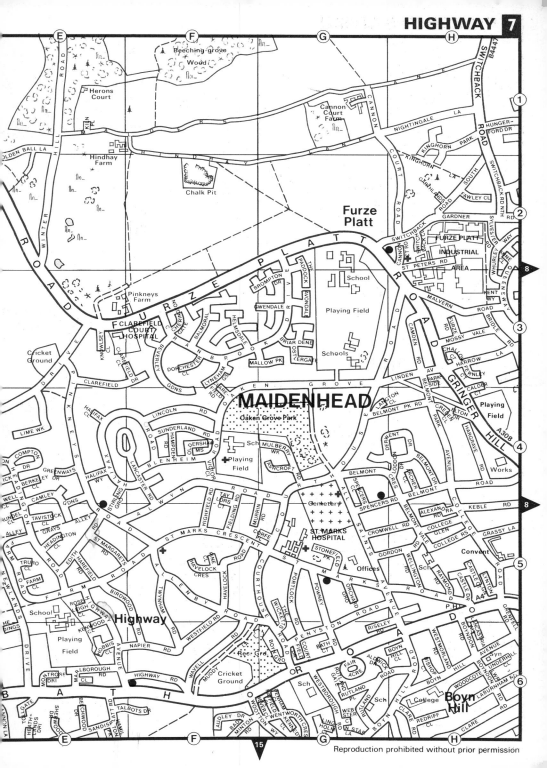

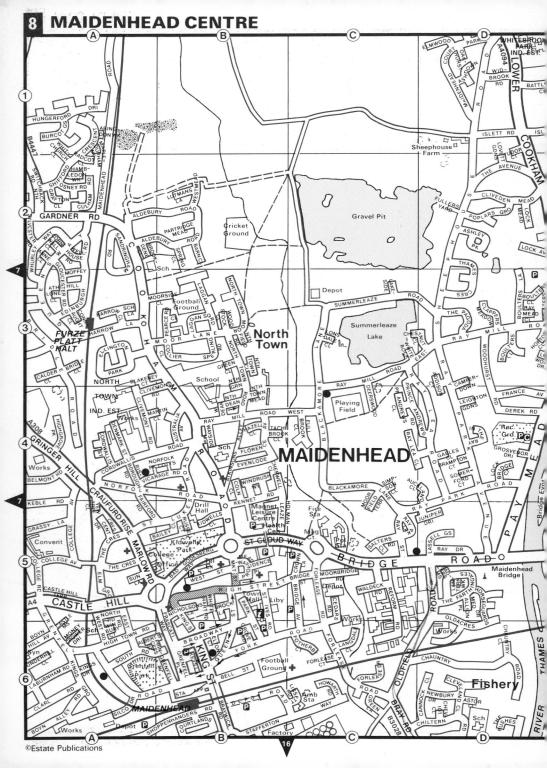

MAIDENHEAD

North Town

Fishery

Gravel Pit

Summerleaze Lake

Cricket Ground

Playing Field

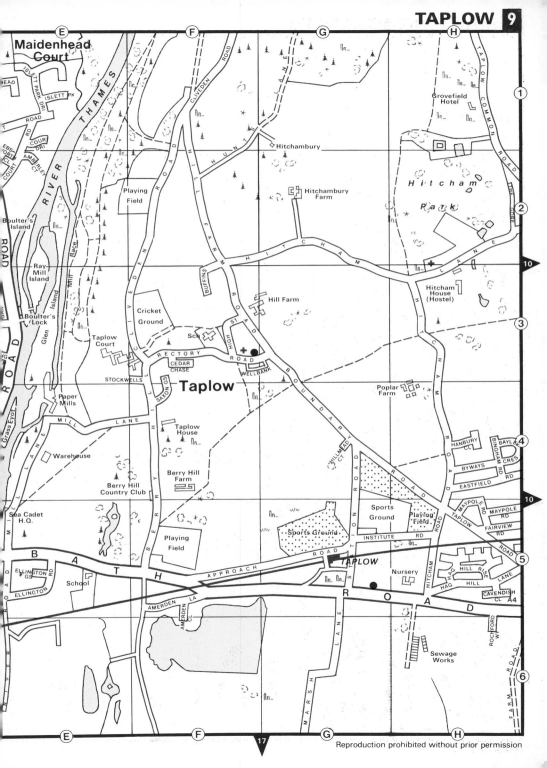

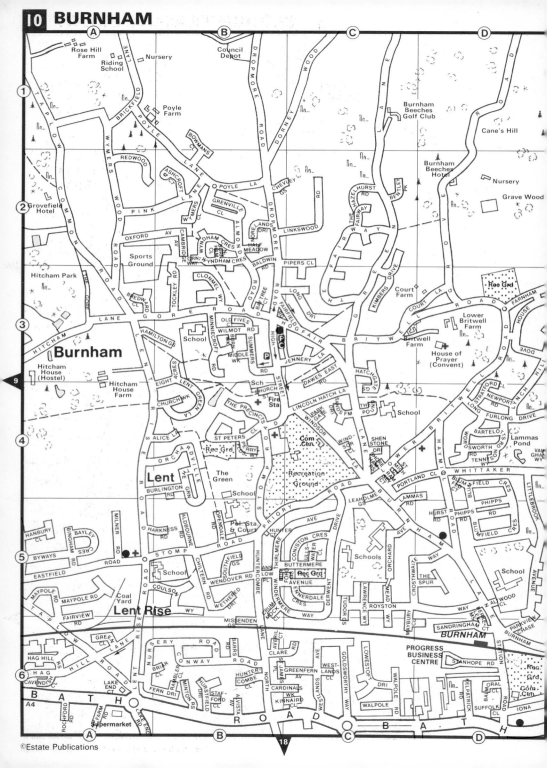

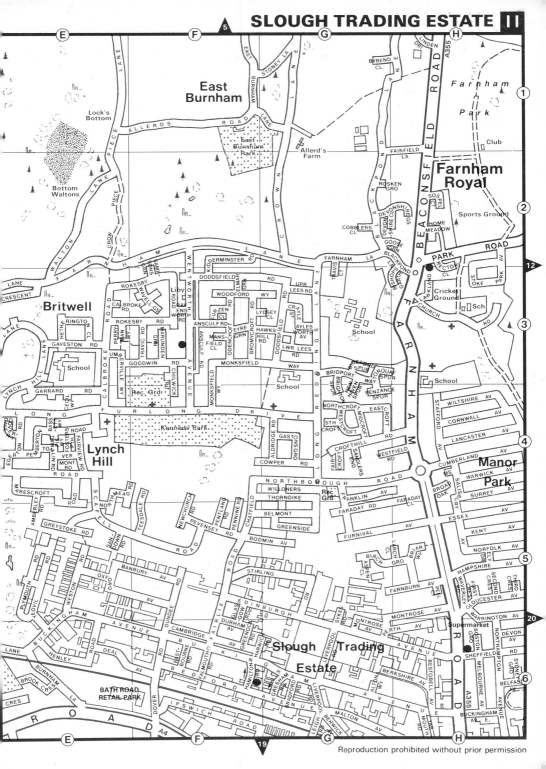

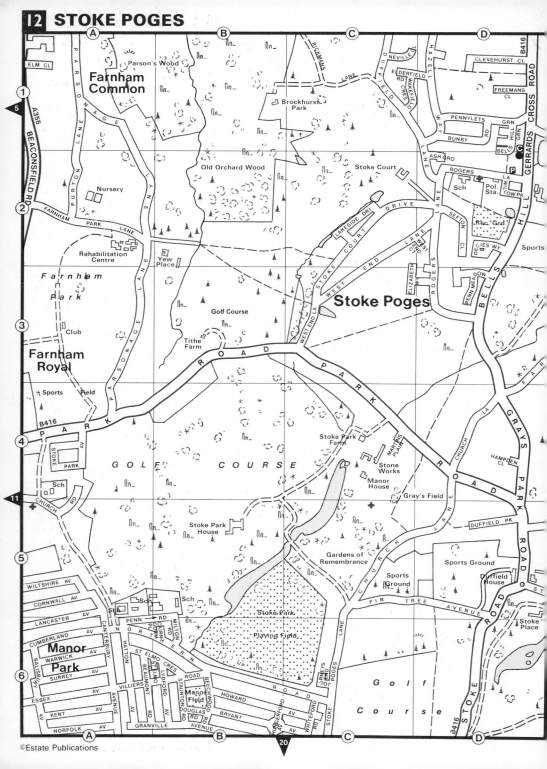

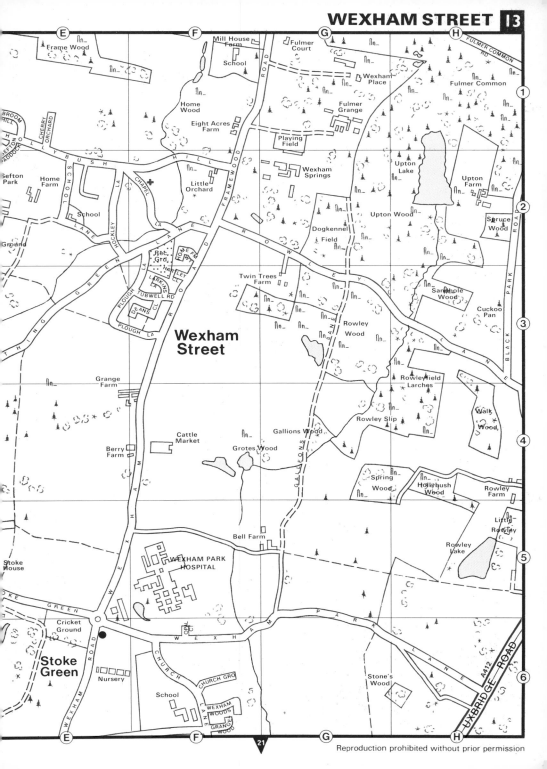

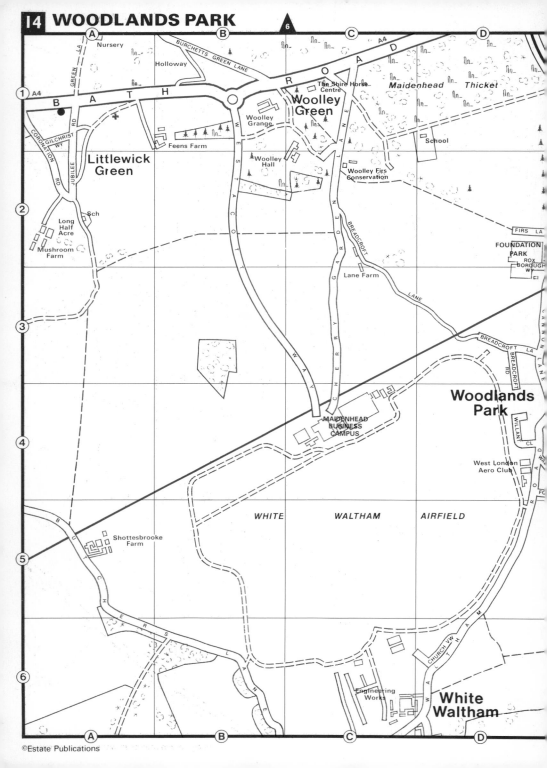

Nursery

BURCHETTS GREEN LANE

Holloway

GREEN LA

A4

A4

The Shire Horse Centre

Maidenhead Thicket

Woolley Green

Woolley Grange

School

B

CORONATION WY

GILCHRIST

JUBILEE RD

Feens Farm

Woolley Hall

Littlewick Green

Woolley Firs Conservation

Sch

Long Half Acre

FIRS LA

FOUNDATION PARK

ROX BOROUGH WY

Mushroom Farm

Lane Farm

CHERRY GARDEN WAY

BREADCROFT

LANE

CANNON LANE

Woodlands Park

BREADCROFT LA

BREADCROFT RD

MAIDENHEAD BUSINESS CAMPUS

WILLAN CL

West London Aero Club

RD WY

FC

WHITE WALTHAM AIRFIELD

B

C

Shottesbrooke Farm

FEE RS

LANE

CHURCH VW

WALTHAM

Engineering Works

White Waltham

MAIDENHEAD

Tittle Row

Cox Green

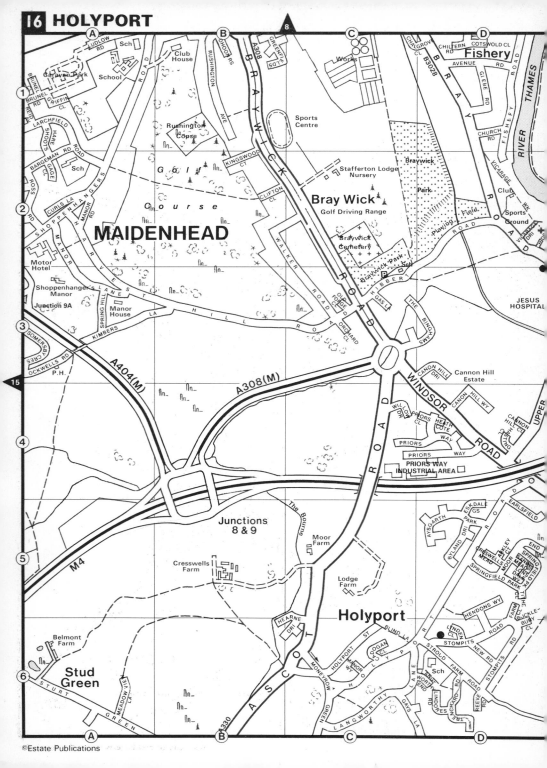

E F 9 G H

1

West Town Farm

LYE MEADS

Sch

A M E R D E N   L A N E

O L D   M A R S H   L A

GLEBE CL

2

Headpile Eyot

Bray Lock

Bray Lock

M4

Bray

BEAUFORT PL

BRAYPARK

R I V E R

GDNS

The Old Mill

Pigeonhill Eyot

Caravan Park

New Thames Bridge

OAK STUBBS LA

MEADOW WAY

HARCOURT ROAD

Sch

FERRY RD

OLD RD

BRAYFIELD

HANOVER TERRACE

HANOVER MEAD

HIGH ST

P

Bray Bridge

BRAY RD

M I L L   L A N E

The Cut

Dorney Reach

HARCOURT

DORNEY REACH RD

3

Hotel

Monkey Island

Weir Bank Stud Farm

M O N K E Y   L A N E

Elm View Farm

18

4

WINDSOR

BRAY CT

COURT CL

Bray Marina

Queen's Eyot

Pit

5

TITHE BARN DRI

BROOK

TITHE BARN DRIVE

BROAD WATER PK

L A N E

River Thames

6

Stroud Farm

Caravan Park

FIFIELD RD

The Guild House

R O A D

Water Oakley Farm

Water Oakley

A308

Oakley Court

E F G H

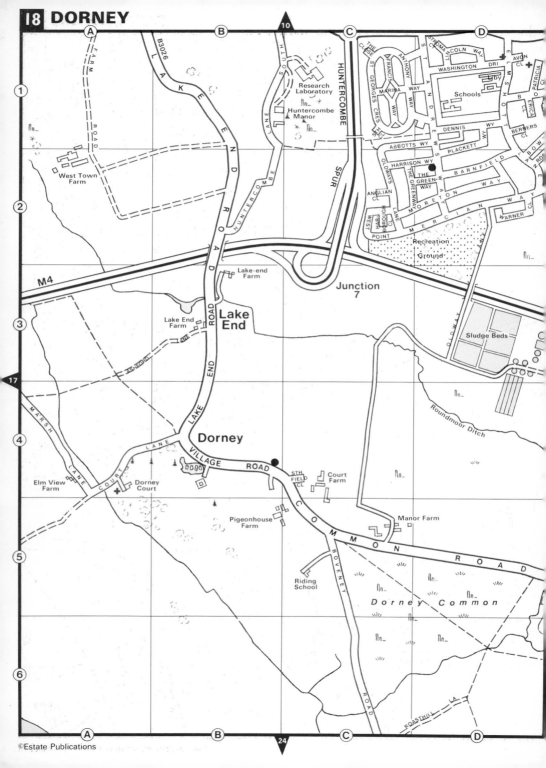

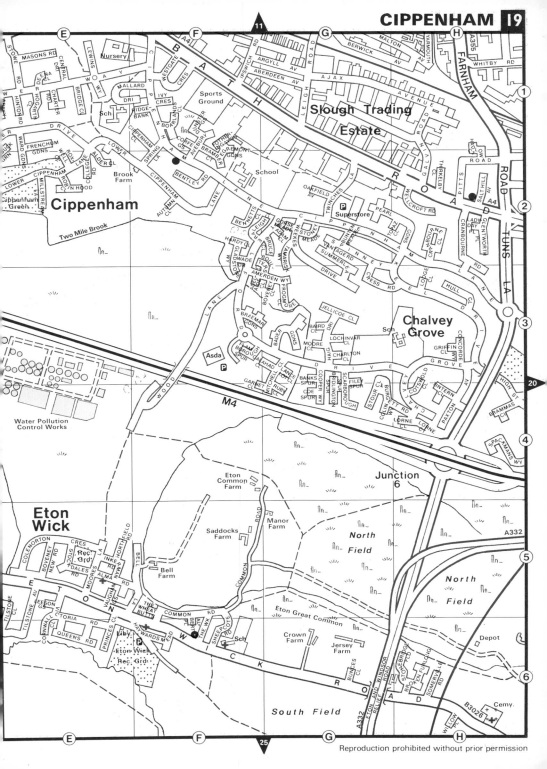

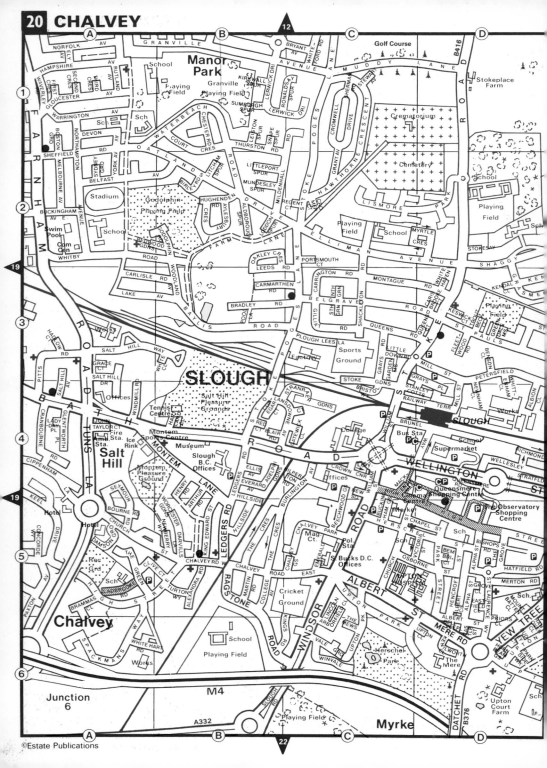

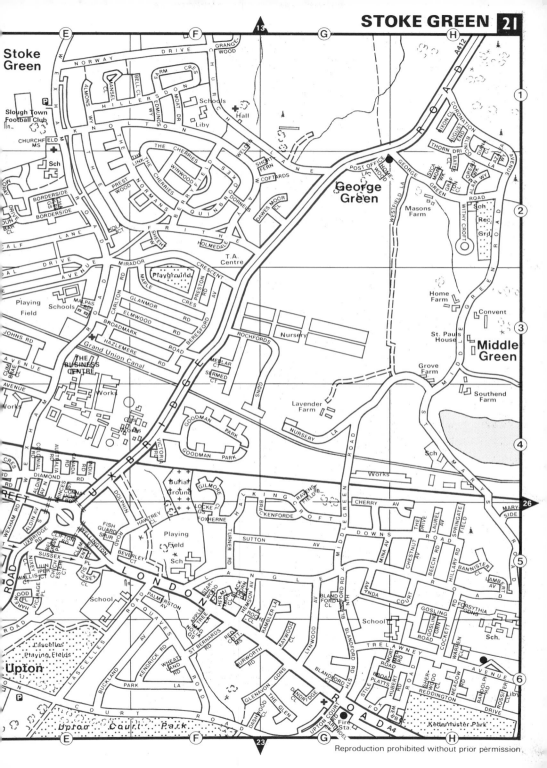

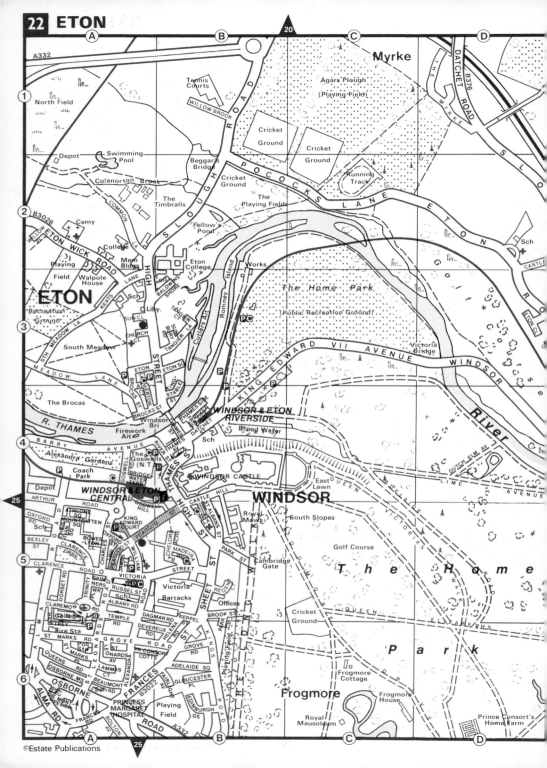

A332

North Field

Depot

Swimming Pool

Colenorton Brook

Tennis Courts

WILLOW BROOK

Beggar's Bridge

The Timbralls

Cricket Ground

The Playing Fields

Myrke

Agars' Plough (Playing Field)

Cricket Ground

Cricket Ground

Running Track

THE MYRKE

DATCHET ROAD

B376

SLOUGH ROAD

POCOCKS LANE

ETON

Sch

CASTLE

B3026

Cemy

ETON WICK ROAD

COMMON

Playing Field

Walpole House

Mem Bldgs

College

Fellow's Pond

Eton College

Works

Romney Island

Cutler's Ait

PC

The Home Park

(Public Recreation Ground)

Victoria Bridge

Golf Course

ETON WICK ROAD

ETON

Recreation Ground

South Meadow

STH MEADOW LA

MEADOW LANE

HIGH STREET

BALDWIN'S SHORE

KEATS LANE

Sch

Liby.

SUN CL.

CHURCH CL

TANGIER LA

SLADE BURY

TANGIER LANE

ETON SQ.

P

BROCAS ST.

STABLE

KING STABLE ST.

P

P

P

P

PC

KING EDWARD VII AVENUE

WINDSOR

ETON GT

The Brocas

R. THAMES

Windsor Bri.

Firework Ait

BARRY AVENUE

RIVER THAMES

WINDSOR & ETON RIVERSIDE

SOUTH SIDE

DATCHET

Sch

Broad Water

River

Alexandra Gardens

P

Coach Park

Depot

ARTHUR ROAD

GOSWELLS

The Goswells (N.T.)

CP

BRIDGE WATER

WINDSOR CASTLE

East Lawn

QUEEN

DUTCH ELM AV.

LIME AVENUE

ADELAIDE AVENUE

VICTORIA'S

WINDSOR & ETON CENTRAL

OXFORD RD

Sch

BEXLEY ST

ATHLONE SQ

MOUNTBATTEN

BOWES LYON

CLARENCE CRES.

CHARLES ST

JAMES ST

WILLIAM

OXFORD RD

KING EDWARD COURT

CASTLE HILL

ST ALBANS ST

CHILDRE

MADERA

WINDSOR

Royal Mews

South Slopes

Golf Course

The Home

CLARENCE ROAD

DORSET RD

TRINITY

CLAREMONT

GOSWELL

COLLEGE

CLARENCE

ST MARKS RD

Fire Sta

P

ST MARKS RD

QUEENS RD

OSBORNE MS

OSBORNE

ALMA RD

MONT

FRANCES

PRINCESS MARGARET HOSPITAL

BOLTON ROAD

A332

VICTORIA

PC

RUSSEL ST

Sch

ALBANY RD

TEMPLE RD

DAGMAR RD

DEVEREUX RD

LEONARDS

LAMMAS

BEAUMONT

ALEXANDRA

B3022

Victoria Barracks

PR CONSORT COTTS

GROVE RD

HELENA RD

KEPPEL ST

GROVE RD

ADELAIDE SQ

Offices

GLOUCESTER PL

EDINBURGH GS

Playing Field

PARK ST

REGENT

SHEET ST

BROOK ST

KINGS ROAD

Playing Field

Cambridge Gate

Cricket Ground

Frogmore

Frogmore Cottage

Frogmore House

Royal Mausoleum

Prince Consort's Home Farm

Park

QUEEN ELIZABETH'S

©Estate Publications

20

25

25

1

2

3

4

5

6

A

B

C

D

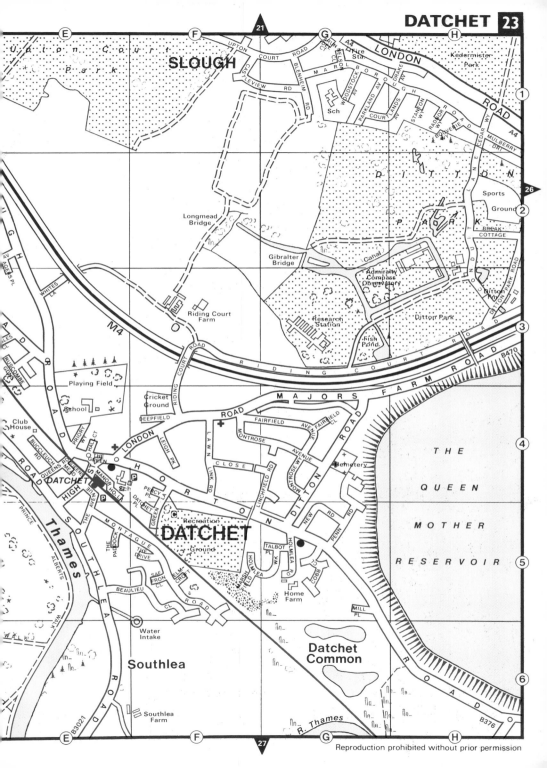

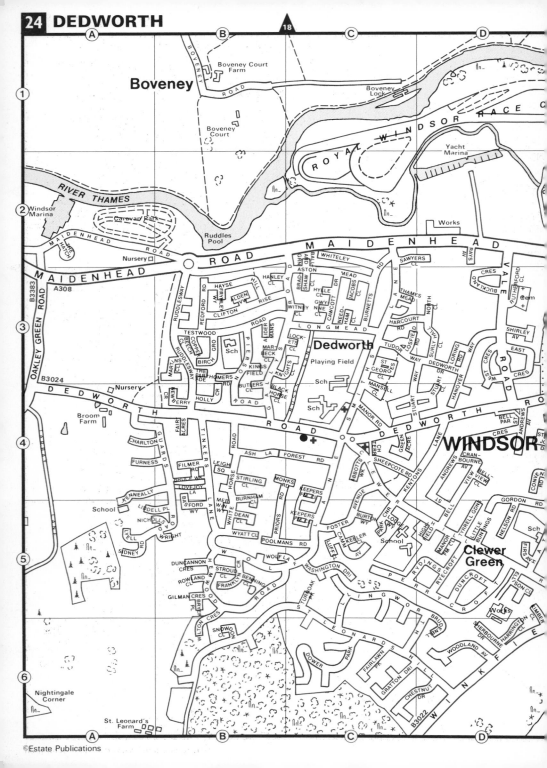

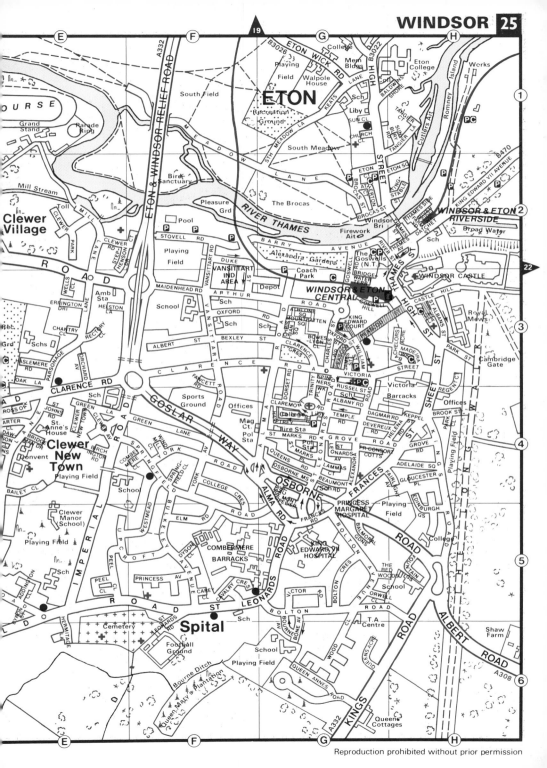

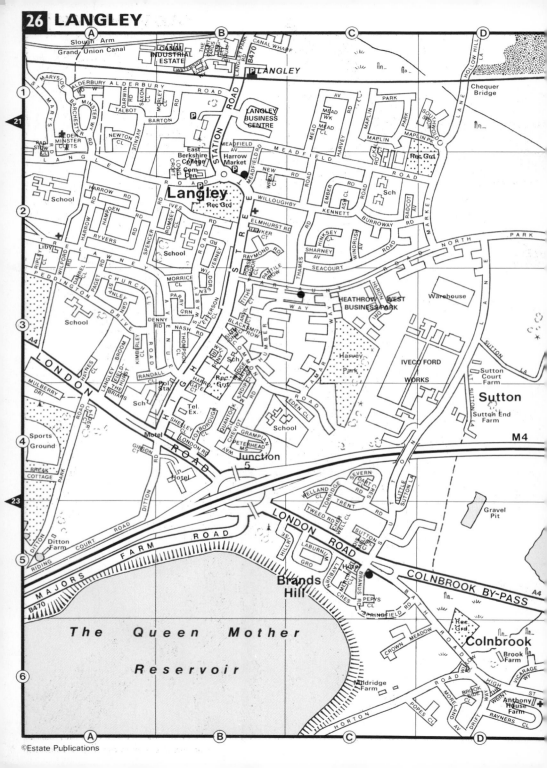

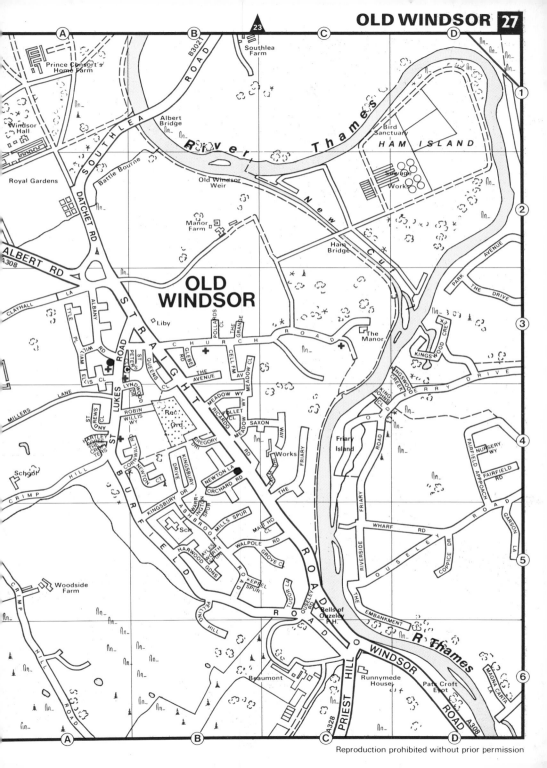

SLOUGH, WINDSOR, MAIDENHEAD

Abbey Clo 19 E1
Abbotts Walk 24 C4
Abbotts Way 18 C1
Aberdeen Av 19 G1
Abingdon Walk 8 A1
Adam Clo 19 G2
Addington Clo 25 E5
Addison Ct 8 D3
Adelaide Clo 19 F3
Adelaide Rd 22 C4
Adelaide Sq 25 H4
Adelphi Gdns 20 B4
Agers Pl 23 E2
Ajax Av 19 G1
Alan Way 21 H2
Albany Rd 25 G4
Albert Clo 20 D5
Albert Pl 19 F6
Albert Rd 25 H5
Albert St,
  Maidenhead 8 A6
Albert St,
  Slough 20 C5
Albert St,
  Windsor 25 F3
Albion Clo 20 D4
Aldborough Spur 20 B2
Aldbourne Rd 10 B5
Aldebury Rd 8 A2
Alden Vw 24 B3
Alder Clo 19 E2
Alderbury Rd 26 A1
Alderbury Rd West 26 A1
Aldin Av N 21 E4
Aldin Av S 21 E5
Aldridge Rd 11 G4
Aldwick Dri 7 G6
Alexandra Rd,
  Maidenhead 7 H5
Alexandra Rd,
  Slough 20 B5
Alexandra Rd,
  Windsor 25 G4
Alice La 10 A4
Alider Mans 24 B3
All Saints Av 7 G4
Allenby Rd 7 F5
Allerds Rd 11 F1
Allkins Ct 22 B6
Alma Rd, Eton Wick 15 E1
Alma Rd, Windsor 25 G4
Almond Rd 10 B2
Almons Way 21 E1
Alpha St 20 D5
Altona Way 11 G6
Altwood Bailey 15 G1
Altwood Clo,
  Burnham 10 D5
Altwood Clo,
  Maidenhead 15 F1
Altwood Dri 15 F1
Altwood Rd 15 E1
Alvista Av 10 B6
Alwyn Rd 7 F5
Amanda Ct 21 G5
Amberley Ct 9 E2
Amberley Rd 11 E4
Amerden Clo 9 F5
Amerden La 9 H5
Amerden Way 19 F3
Anglian Clo 18 C2
Anne Clo 8 A2
Ansculf Rd 11 F3
Anslow Pl 10 B5
Anthony Way 18 C1
Anvil Ct 26 B3
Applecroft 15 G3
Appletree La 21 F5
Approach Rd 9 F5
Arborfield Clo 20 C6
Archer Clo 7 H4
Argyll Av 19 G1
Arkley Ct 16 D5
Arlington Clo 20 B5
Arthur Rd, Slough 20 B5
Arthur Rd, Windsor 25 F3
Arundel Clo 7 E5
Arundel Ct 21 G6
Ascot Rd 16 B6
Ash Clo 26 C2
Ash Gro 12 D2
Ash La 24 B4
Ashbourne Gro 15 G3

Ashcroft Ct 10 B2
Ashcroft Rd 7 G4
Ashdown 8 D1
Ashford La 18 A3
Ashley Pk 8 D2
Ashton Pl 15 E1
Aspen Clo 11 G5
Aston Mead 24 C3
Astor Clo 8 D6
Atherton Ct 22 A4
Athlone Clo 8 A3
Athlone Sq 25 G3
Atkinsons All 8 B4
Auckland Clo 8 D4
Audley Dri 7 F6
August End 21 H1
Austins Gate 6 D4
Australia Av 8 B4
Australia Rd 21 E4
Autumn Clo 19 F2
Autumn Walk 15 E1
Avebury 19 F2
Avenue Rd 16 D1
Averil Ct 10 B6
Avon Clo 18 D1
Avondale 7 G3
Aylesbury Cres 20 B2
Aylesworth Av 11 G3
Aysgarth Pk 16 D5
Azalea Way 21 H2

Bachelors Acre 25 H3
Bad Godesberg Way 8 B5
Bader Gdns 19 G3
Badger Clo 15 H2
Badminton Rd 7 F6
Bailey Clo,
  Maidenhead 8 B5
Bailey Clo,
  Windsor 25 E4
Baird Clo 19 G3
Bakers La 6 D4
Baldwin Rd 10 B2
Baldwins Shore 22 B3
Ballard Grn 24 C2
Balmoral 7 F3
Balmoral Clo 10 B6
Balmoral Gdns 25 G5
Banbury Av 11 E5
Banks Spur 19 G3
Bannard Rd 15 E1
Bannister Clo 21 H5
Barchester Rd 26 A1
Bardney Clo 15 H3
Bargeman Rd 16 A2
Barn Clo 8 B2
Barn Dri 15 E2
Barnfield 18 D2
Barrs Rd 10 B6
Barry Av 25 G2
Bartelotts Rd 10 D4
Barton Rd 26 A1
Basford Way 24 B5
Bassett Way 11 E4
Bates Clo 21 H2
Bath Ct 7 G6
Bath Rd, Langley 26 C5
Bath Rd,
  Littlewick Grn 14 A1
Bath Rd, Slough 20 A4
Bath Rd, Taplow 9 E5
Battlemead Clo 8 D1
Bay Tree Ct 10 B3
Bayley Cres 10 A5
Baylis Rd 20 B3
Beaconsfield Rd 11 H2
Beaufort Pl 17 E2
Beaulieu Clo 23 E5
Beaumont Clo 15 E3
Beaumont Rd,
  Slough 12 A6
Beaumont Rd,
  Windsor 25 G4
Bedford Av 11 F6
Bedford Clo 15 E3
Beech Rd 21 H5
Beechwood Dri 7 E6
Beechwood Gdns 20 C5
Beechwood Rd 12 B6
Belfast Av 10 D4
Belgrave Pl 8 B4
Belgrave Rd 20 C3
Bell Clo 21 F1
Bell La 19 F5
Bell Par 24 D4
Bell St 8 B6
Bell Vw 24 D5
Bellevue Pl 20 D6
Bells Hill 12 D3

Bells Hill Grn 12 D1
Bellview Clo 24 D4
Bellvue Pl 20 D6
Belmont 11 G5
Belmont Cres 7 G4
Belmont Dri 7 H4
Belmont Park Av 7 H3
Belmont Park Rd 7 G4
Belmont Vale 7 H5
Bembridge Ct 20 D5
Bennetts Clo 19 F2
Benning Ct 24 B5
Benson Clo 20 D3
Bentley Pk 10 C2
Bentley Rd 19 F2
Beresford Av 21 F3
Berkeley Clo 7 E4
Berkeley Ms 10 D5
Berkshire Av 11 H6
Berners Clo 18 D1
Berry Hill 9 F5
Berryfield 21 F1
Berwick Av 19 G1
Bestobell Av 11 H6
Beverley Cr 21 F5
Beverley Gdns 7 F3
Bexley St 25 F3
Bideford Spur 11 G3
Bingham Rd 10 A5
Birch Gro, Slough 11 G5
Birch Gro, Windsor 24 B3
Birchington Rd 25 E4
Birdwood Rd 7 E5
Birley Rd 20 B2
Bishop Ct 7 H6
Bishops Garth 11 H3
Bishops Rd 20 D5
Bissley Dri 15 E3
Bix La 6 D4
Black Horse Clo 24 B4
Black Park Rd 13 H3
Blackamore La 8 C4
Blackpond La 11 G2
Blacksmith Row 26 B3
Blackthorn Dell 21 F5
Blair Rd 20 B4
Blakeney Ct 8 A3
Blandford Clo 21 G5
Blandford Ct 21 G6
Blandford Rd Nth 21 G5
Blandford Rd Sth 21 G6
Blenheim Rd,
  Maidenhead 7 F4
Blenheim Rd,
  Slough 23 G1
Blinco La 21 H1
Blind La 16 C6
Blomfield Rd 15 E1
Blumfield Ct 10 D4
Blumfield Cres 10 D4
Boardlands Clo 19 F1
Bodmin Av 11 F5
Bolton Av 25 G5
Bolton Cres 25 G5
Bolton Rd 25 G5
Bone Av 25 G6
Boston Gro 20 A1
Boulters Clo,
  Maidenhead 8 D3
Boulters Clo,
  Slough 19 G3
Boulters Grn 8 D3
Boulters La 8 D3
Boundary Rd 25 G5
Bourne Av 20 A5
Bourne Rd 20 A5
Bourne Way 23 H1
Boveney Clo 19 G3
Boveney New Rd 19 E5
Boveney Rd 18 C5
Bower Way 18 D1
Bowes Lyon Clo 25 G3
Bowmans Clo 10 B1
Bowyer Dri 18 D1
Boyn Gro 7 G6
Boyn Hill Av 7 H6
Boyn Hill Clo 7 H6
Boyn Hill Rd 7 G6
Boyn Valley Rd 15 G1
Boyndon Rd 7 H6
Bradford Rd 11 G6
Bradley Rd 20 B3
Bradshaw Clo 24 C3
Braemar Gdns 19 F3
Bramber Ct 19 F1
Bramble Dri 15 E1

Bramley Clo 15 G3
Brammas Clo 20 A5
Brampton Ct 8 D4
Brands Rd 26 C5
Bray Clo 17 E3
Bray Rd 16 D1
Braybank 17 E2
Brayfield Rd 17 E3
Braywick Rd 16 B1
Breadcroft La 14 C2
Breadcroft Rd 14 D3
Break Cottage 23 H2
Bredward Clo 10 A3
Briar Clo 10 A6
Briar Dene 7 G3
Briar Way 11 H5
Brickfield La 10 Al
Bridge Av 8 C5
Bridge Clo 19 E1
Bridge Rd 8 C5
Bridge St 8 C5
Bridgeman Dri 25 E4
Bridgewater Ct 26 B3
Bridgewater Ter 25 G3
Bridle Clo 8 A3
Bridle Rd 8 A3
Bridlington Spur 19 G3
Bridport Way 11 G3
Brighton Spur 11 G3
Brill Clo 15 G3
Bristol Way 20 C4
Britwell Rd 10 C3
Broad Clo 11 H4
Broad Platts 21 G6
Broadmark Rd 21 E3
Broadwater Park 17 F5
Broadway 8 B6
Brocas St 22 A4
Brock La 8 B5
Broken Furlong 19 H6
Brompton Dri 7 G3
Bromycroft Rd 11 F3
Brook Cres 11 E6
Brook St 25 H4
Brookdene Clo 8 A2
Brookside 18 D6
Broom Hill 13 E1
Bruce Clo 19 G2
Bruce Walk 24 B4
Brudenell 8 B6
Brunel Rd 15 H1
Brunel Rd 15 H1
Brunel Way 20 C4
Bryant Av 12 B6
Bryer Pl 24 B5
Buccleuch Rd 23 E4
Buckingham Av 11 E6
Buckingham Av E 20 A2
Buckingham Gdns 20 C5
Buckland Av 21 E6
Buckland Cres 24 D3
Bucklebury Clo 16 D5
Buffins 9 F3
Bulkeley Av 25 F5
Bunby Rd 12 D1
Bunces Clo 19 G6
Bunten Meade 19 G2
Burchetts Green La 6 A5
Burchetts Green Rd 6 A5
Burcot Gdns 8 A1
Burford Gdns 10 C5
Burgett Rd 19 G4
Burlington Av 20 C4
Burlington Rd 10 A4
Burn Walk 10 B3
Burnetts Rd 24 C3
Burnham Clo 24 B4
Burnham La 11 G6
Burroway Rd 26 C2
Burton Way 24 C5
Butchers La 14 A5
Butlers Clo 24 B4
Buttermere Av 10 C5
Byland Dri 16 D5
Byron Ct 25 E5
Byways 10 A5

Cadogan Clo 16 C6
Cadwell Dri 15 H3
Cairngorm Pl 12 B6
Cairnbroke Rd 8 A3
Calder Clo 19 G6
Calder Ct,
  Langley 26 A4
Calder Ct,
  Maidenhead 7 H4
Cambridge Av,
  Burnham 10 B2

Cambridge Av,
  Slough 11 F6
Camden Rd 7 H3
Camley Gdns 7 E4
Camley Park Dri 6 D4
Camm Av 24 C5
Camperdown 8 D2
Canada Rd 21 E4
Canal Wharf 26 B1
Cannock Clo 8 D6
Cannon Court Rd 7 G1
Cannon Hill Clo 16 D4
Cannon La 15 E1
Canon Hill Dri 16 D3
Canon Hill Way 16 D4
Canterbury Av 12 A6
Cardinals Walk 10 B6
Carey Clo 25 F5
Carisbrook Clo 15 G1
Carisbrooke Ct 20 D3
Carlisle Rd 20 A3
Carlton Rd 21 E3
Carmarthen Rd 20 B3
Carrington Rd 20 C3
Carter Clo 25 E4
Castle Av 22 D2
Castle Ct 7 H5
Castle Dri 7 H5
Castle Hill Ter 8 A5
Castle Hill,
  Maidenhead 8 A5
Castle Hill,
  Windsor 25 H3
Castle Mews 8 A6
Castle St 20 D6
Castleview Rd 23 F1
Cavalry Cres 25 F5
Cavendish Clo 9 H5
Cawcott Dri 24 C3
Cecil Way 11 E4
Cedar Chase 9 F3
Cedar Way 23 H1
Cedars Rd 8 C5
Central Dri 19 E1
Chalgrove Clo 16 C1
Challow Ct 7 H3
Chalvey Gdns 20 C5
Chalvey Pk 20 C5
Chalvey Rd E 20 B5
Chalvey Rd W 20 B5
Chantry La 25 E3
Chapel La 13 F2
Chapel St 20 C5
Charles Gdns 21 E2
Charles St 25 G3
Charlton 24 A4
Charlton Clo 19 G3
Charter Rd 19 E1
Chatfield 11 F5
Chatsworth Clo 15 G1
Chauntry Clo 8 D6
Chauntry Rd 8 D6
Cheniston Grn 6 D5
Cherington Gate 7 F3
Cherry Av 23 G1
Cherry Garden La 14 C4
Cherry Orchard 13 E1
Cherwell Clo,
  Langley 26 C5
Cherwell Clo,
  Maidenhead 8 B4
Chester Rd 20 B1
Chestnut Av 21 H5
Chestnut Clo 8 D3
Chestnut Dri 19 H4
Cheviot Clo 8 D6
Cheviot Rd 26 B4
Chevley Gdns 10 B2
Chichester Ct 21 E5
Chiltern Rd,
  Maidenhead 8 D6
Chiltern Rd,
  Slough 10 B5
Chilwick Rd 11 F3
Christian Sq 25 G3
Church Clo 22 A3
Church Dri 16 D2
Church Gro 13 F6
Church La, Bray 17 E2
Church La, Slough 21 F1
Church La,
  Stoke Poges 12 C5
Church La, Windsor 25 H3
Church Rd,
  Maidenhead 16 D1
Church Rd, Slough 11 H3
Church St, Burnham 10 B3
Church St, Chalvey 20 A5
Church St, Slough 20 C5

28

Church Ter 24 C4
Church Vw 14 D6
Church Walk 10 B4
Churchfield Mews 21 E1
Churchill Rd 26 A3
Cippenham Clo 19 F1
Cippenham La 19 F1
Clappers Meadow 8 D3
Clare Rd, Maidenhead 7 H6
Clare Rd, Slough 10 B6
Clarefield Clo 7 F3
Clarefield Dri 7 E3
Clarefield Rd 7 F4
Claremont Rd 25 G4
Clarence Cres 25 G3
Clarence Rd 25 F3
Clements Clo 21 E5
Clevehurst Clo 12 D1
Cleveland Clo 8 D6
Clewer Av 25 E4
Clewer Ct 25 E2
Clewer Hill Rd 24 C4
Clewer New Town 25 E4
Clewer Pk 25 E2
Clewer Rd 25 E2
Clifton Clo 16 B2
Clifton Rise 24 B3
Clifton Road 21 E5
Clive Ct 20 A5
Cliveden Mead 8 D2
Cliveden Rd 9 F3
Clivemont Rd 8 A4
Clonmel Way 10 B3
Cobb Clo 23 G5
Cobblers Clo 11 G2
Cockett Rd 21 H5
Coe Spur 19 G4
Coftards 21 G2
Colenorton Cres 19 E5
Colin Way 19 G4
College Av, Chalvey 20 B5
College Av, Maidenhead 8 A5
College Cres 25 F4
College Glen 7 H5
College Rise 7 H5
College Rd, Maidenhead 7 H5
College Rd, Slough 19 E2
Collier Clo 8 B3
Coln Clo 8 B4
Colnbrook By-Pass 26 C5
Colonial Rd 21 E4
Combemere Clo 25 F4
Common La 22 A2
Common Rd, Eton Wick 19 F5
Common Rd, Langley 26 B3
Common Rd, Slough 18 C5
Compton Dri 7 E4
Concorde Way 19 H3
Conduit La 23 H3
Conegar Ct 20 B4
Coniston Cres 10 C5
Connaught Clo 8 A3
Connaught Rd 21 E4
Conningsby Clo 15 H3
Convent Rd 24 D4
Conway Rd 10 B6
Cooper Way 19 G3
Copper Beech Clo 24 B3
Copthorn Clo 15 E2
Cordwallis Rd 8 A4
Cordwallis St 8 A4
Corfe Gdns 19 F1
Corfe Pl 7 G5
Cornwall Av 11 H1
Cornwall Clo, Maidenhead 8 A2
Cornwall Clo, Slough 19 E5
Coronation Av 21 H1
Coronation Rd 14 A1
Cotswold Clo, Maidenhead 16 D1
Cotswold Clo, Slough 19 H4
Coulson Way 10 A5
Court Cres 20 B1
Court Dri 9 E1
Court Clo 17 E4
Court La, Burnham 10 C3
Court La, Slough 18 A4
Court Rd 9 E2
Courtfield Dri 7 G6
Courthouse Rd 7 G5
Courtlands 8 B6
Courtlands Av 23 G1
Coverdale Way 11 E4
Cowper Rd 11 G4
Cox Green La 15 F3
Cox Green Rd 15 G2
Cranbourne Av 24 D4
Cranbourne Clo 19 H2
Cranbourne Rd 19 H2
Cranbrook Dri 7 F3
Craufurd Rise 8 A4
Crayle St 11 G3
Creden Clo 7 H4
Crescent Dri 8 A5
Cress Rd 19 G3
Cresswells Mead 16 D5
Crofthill Rd 11 G4
Cromer Ct 20 C2
Cromwell Dri 20 C1
Cromwell Rd 7 G5
Cross Oak 25 E4
Crosthwaite Way 10 C5
Crow Piece 11 E2
Crown Corner 20 C4
Crown La, Maidenhead 8 C5
Crown La, Slough 11 G2
Crown Meadow 26 C6
Crummock Clo 10 B5
Culham Rd 8 A2
Culley Way 15 E2
Cumberland Av 11 H4
Cumbrae Clo 21 E3
Cumbria Clo 15 G2
Curls La 16 A2
Curls Rd 15 H2

Dagmar Rd 25 G4
Damson Gro 20 A5
Dandridge Clo 21 G6
Darlings La 6 D3
Darrel Clo 26 A3
Dart Clo 26 C4
Darvills La 20 B5
Darwin Rd 26 A1
Dashwood Clo 21 F6
Datchet Pl 23 F5
Datchet Rd 22 D1
Datchet St 25 H2
Davids Clo 15 F2
Dawes East Rd 10 C3
Dawes Moor Clo 21 G2
Dawson Clo 25 E4
Deal Av 11 E6
Dean Clo 24 B5
Deans Clo 13 F3
Decies Way 12 D2
Dedworth Dri 24 D3
Dedworth Rd 24 C4
Deena Clo 19 E1
Deepfield 23 F4
Deerswood 8 C4
Denham Clo 7 G6
Denmark St 8 A4
Dennis Way 18 D1
Denny Rd 26 A3
Depot Rd 8 B6
Derek Rd 8 D4
Derwent Dri, Maidenhead 7 H4
Derwent Dri, Slough 10 C5
Desborough Cres 15 G1
Devereux Rd 25 G4
Devon Av 20 A1
Devonshire Clo 11 G2
Devonshire Gdns 11 G2
Dhoon Rise 16 B1
Diamond Rd 21 E4
Diana Clo 21 H2
Disraeli Ct 26 C5
Ditton Park Rd 26 A5
Ditton Rd, Datchet 23 G5
Ditton Rd, Langley 26 A5
Doddsfield Rd 11 F3
Dolphin Rd 21 E4
Dorchester Clo 7 F3
Dornels 21 F2
Dorney Reach Rd 17 G3
Dorney Wood 10 B1
Dorset Rd 25 G4
Douglas Rd 12 B6
Dove House Cres 10 D3
Dover Rd 11 F6
Dower Pk 24 C6
Downs Rd 21 G5
Drake Av 23 H1
Drift Way 26 D6
Dropmore Rd 10 B1
Dudley Ct 20 D6
Duffield La 12 C1
Duffield Pk 12 D5
Duke St 25 F2
Dunbar Clo 21 E2
Duncannon Cres 24 B5
Duncroft 24 D5
Dundee Rd 11 F5
Dungrove Hill La 6 A2
Dunholme End 15 H3
Dunster Gdns 19 F1
Durham Av 11 F6
Dutch Elm Av 22 D4
Dyson Clo 25 F5

Earlsfield 16 D5
East Burnham La 11 F1
East Cres 24 D3
East Rd 8 A5
Eastbourne Rd 11 F6
Eastcroft 11 G4
Eastfield Clo 20 D5
Eastfield Rd 10 A5
Ebsworth Clo 9 E2
Eden Clo 26 C4
Edinburgh Av 11 F5
Edinburgh Gdns 25 H5
Edinburgh Rd 8 A3
Edith Rd 7 E5
Edmunds Way 21 F1
Egerton Rd 11 E4
Egremont Gdns 19 F2
Eight Acres 10 B3
Elder Way 26 B1
Elderfield Rd 12 C1
Elizabeth Way 12 C3
Elliman Av 20 C2
Ellington Gdns 9 E5
Ellington Pk 8 A3
Ellington Rd 9 E5
Ellis Av 20 B4
Ellison Clo 24 D5
Elm Clo 12 A1
Elm Gro 8 A5
Elm Rd 25 F5
Elmar Grn 11 F3
Elmcroft 23 F5
Elmhurst Rd 26 B2
Elmshott La 18 D1
Elmwood 8 D1
Elmwood Rd 21 E3
Elton Ct 8 B6
Elton Dri 7 H4
Ely Av 20 A1
Ember Rd 26 C2
Emerald Ct 20 C5
Ennerdale Cres 10 C5
Erica Clo 18 D1
Errington Dri 25 E3
Eskdale Gdns 16 D5
Essex Av 11 H5
Eton Clo 22 D3
Eton Ct 22 A3
Eton Rd 22 D2
Eton Sq 22 B3
Eton Wick Rd 19 E5
Eton and Windsor Relief Rd 25 F2
Evenlode 8 B4
Everard Av 20 B4
Eyre Grn 11 F3

Fair Acre 7 G6
Fairacres 24 B4
Faircroft 11 G4
Fairfield Av 23 F4
Fairfield Clo 23 G4
Fairfield La 11 H1
Fairfield Rd 10 B3
Fairford Rd 8 A4
Fairlawn Pl 24 C6
Fairlea 15 F3
Fairlie Rd 11 F6
Fairlight Av 25 G4
Fairview Rd, Lent Rise 10 A5
Fairview Rd, Lynch Hill 11 E4
Falmouth Rd 11 F6
Fane Way 15 H1
Faraday Clo 11 H4
Faraday Rd 11 G5
Farm Clo, Holyport 16 D5
Farm Clo, Maidenhead 7 E5
Farm Cres 21 F1
Farm La 20 B2
Farm Rd, Maidenhead 7 E5
Farm Rd, Slough 10 A6
Farm Yd 25 H2
Farmers Clo 15 E2
Farmers Way 15 E2
Farnburn Av 11 H5
Farnham La 11 E3
Farnham Park La 12 A2
Farnham Rd 11 H3
Farthing Green La 12 D3
Fawcett Rd 25 F3
Fawley Clo 7 H2
Fern Dri 10 A6
Fernley Ct 7 H3
Ferry Rd 17 E2
Fieldhurst 26 A3
Fielding Rd 7 F5
Fifield Rd 17 F6
Filey Spur 19 G3
Filmer Rd 24 B4
Finch Ct 15 H1
Fir Tree Av 12 C5
Firs Av 24 D5
Firs La 14 D2
First Cres 20 A1
Fishery Rd 16 D1
Fishguard Spur 21 E5
Flamborough Spur 19 F3
Fleetwood Rd 20 D3
Florence Av 8 B4
Foliejohn Way 14 D4
Folkestone Ct 26 B4
Fontwell Clo 7 E4
Forest Rd 24 C4
Forlease Ct 8 C6
Forlease Dri 8 C6
Forlease Rd 8 C5
Forsythia Gdns 21 H5
Foster Av 24 C5
Fosters Path 11 E4
Fotherby Ct 8 C6
Fotheringay Gdns 19 F1
Fountain Gdns 25 H5
Fox Rd 21 G6
Foxborough Clo 26 B4
Foxherne 21 F5
Framewood Rd 13 F2
France Av 8 D4
Frances Rd 25 G5
Frances St 25 G4
Francis Way 18 C1
Franklin Av 11 G4
Franklyn Cres 24 B5
Frascati Way 8 B5
Freemans Clo 12 D1
Frenchum Gdns 19 E1
Frogmore Clo 19 G3
Frogmore Dri 22 B5
Frymley Way 24 B3
Fullbrook Clo 8 C4
Fullers Yard 8 D2
Fulmer Common Rd 13 H1
Furness 24 A4
Furnival Av 11 G5
Furrow Way 15 E2
Furze Platt Rd 7 E3
Furze Rd 7 H3
Furzen Clo 11 F3

Gables Clo, Datchet 23 E3
Gables Clo, Maidenhead 8 D4
Gage Clo 16 A2
Gainsborough Dri 15 H3
Galahad Clo 19 G3
Galleons La 13 G4
Gallys Rd 24 B4
Galvin Rd 19 H2
Garden Clo 15 E1
Garden Mews 20 C3
Gardner Rd 8 A2
Garnet Clo 19 F3
Garrard Rd 11 E4
Garthlands 7 H2
Gas La 16 C3
Gascons Gro 11 G4
Gatewick Clo 20 C4
Gaveston Rd 11 E3
Gays La 16 C6
George Green Rd 21 H2
Gerrards Cross Rd 12 D2
Gibson Ct 26 A4
Gilchrist Way 14 A1
Gilliat Rd 20 C3
Gilman Cres 24 B5
Gilmore Clo 21 F4
Gladstone Way 19 F2
Glanmor Rd 21 F3
Glasgow Rd 11 F5
Glebe Clo 17 G2
Glebe Rd 16 D1
Glenavon Gdns 21 G6
Glentworth Pl 19 H2
Gloucester Av 20 A1
Gloucester Pl 25 H4
Gloucester Rd 8 A3
Godolphin Rd 20 B2
Golden Ball La 7 E2
Goldsworthy Way 10 C6
Goodman Pk 21 F4
Goodwin Rd 11 F3
Goose Grn 11 G2
Gordon Rd, Maidenhead 7 G5
Gordon Rd, Windsor 24 D5
Gore Rd 10 A3
Gorsemeade 19 G2
Goslar Way 25 F4
Gosling Grn 21 H6
Gosling Rd 21 H5
Goswell Hill 25 G3
Goswell Rd 25 G3
Grace Ct 20 A3
Grafton Clo, Maidenhead 8 A2
Grafton Clo, Slough 21 H2
Graham Clo 15 G1
Grampian Way 26 B4
Grangewood 21 F1
Grant Av 20 C2
Granville Av 20 A1
Grasmere Av 20 D3
Grassy La 7 H5
Gratton Dri 24 C6
Grays All 6 D5
Grays Park Rd 12 D4
Grays Pl 20 C3
Grays Rd 20 C3
Great Hill Cres 15 F1
Green Acre 24 C4
Green Clo, Maidenhead 8 B3
Green Clo, Slough 10 A6
Green La, Burnham 10 C3
Green La, Datchet 23 F5
Green La, Littlewick Grn 14 A1
Green La, Maidenhead 8 C6
Green La, Windsor 25 E4
Greendale Mews 20 D3
Greenfern Av 10 C6
Greenfields 16 B1
Greenock Rd 11 F6
Greenside 11 G5
Greenway 10 B2
Greenways Dri 7 E4
Grenfell Av 8 B6
Grenfell Pl 8 B6
Grenfell Rd 8 A5
Grenville Clo 10 B2
Gresham Rd 11 G6
Greystoke Rd 11 E5
Griffin Clo, Maidenhead 16 A1
Griffin Clo, Slough 19 H3
Gringer Hill 7 H3
Grosvenor Dri 8 D4
Grove Clo 20 D5
Grove Rd, Maidenhead 8 B6
Grove Rd, Slough 10 D3
Grove Rd, Windsor 25 H4
Guards Rd 24 B4
Gwendale 7 G3
Gwent Clo 15 F2
Gwynne Clo 24 C3

Haddon Rd 15 G1
Hadlow Ct 19 H2
Hag Hill La 9 H5
Hag Hill Rise 9 H5
Haig Dri 19 G3
Half Meadow 10 B2
Halifax Clo 7 E4
Halifax Rd 7 E4
Halifax Way 7 E4
Halkingcroft 21 F5
Hall Ct 23 E4
Hall Place La 6 A5
Hambledon Walk 8 A2
Hamilton Gdns 10 A3
Hamilton Pk 7 E6
Hamilton Rd 11 F6
Hampden Clo 12 D4
Hampden Rd, Langley 26 A2
Hampden Rd, Maidenhead 7 F4
Hampshire Av 20 A1
Hanbury Clo 9 H4
Hanley Clo 24 B3
Hanover Clo 20 D6
Hanover Mead 17 E3
Hanover Way 24 D3
Harborough Clo 18 C2
Harcourt Clo 17 G3
Harcourt Rd, Bray 17 G3
Harcourt Rd, Windsor 24 C3
Hardwick Clo 7 E4
Hardy Clo 19 F2
Hare Shoots 16 A1
Harefield Rd 7 E5
Harewood Pl 21 E5
Hargrave Rd 7 H4
Harkness Rd 10 A5
Harrington Clo 24 D6
Harrison Way 18 C2
Harrogate Ct 26 B3
Harrow Clo 8 A3
Harrow La 7 H3
Harrow Rd 26 A2
Hartland Clo 20 B4
Hartley Clo 13 F3
Harvest Hill Rd 16 A2
Harvey Rd 26 C2
Harwich Rd 11 F6
Haslemere Rd 25 E3
Hasting Clo 16 D4
Hatch La 24 D5
Hatchgate Gdns 10 C3
Hatfield Clo 7 G6
Hatfield Rd 20 D5
Hatton Av 12 A6
Havelock Cres 7 F5
Havelock Rd 7 F5
Hawker Ct 26 B2

Hawkshill Rd 11 G3
Hawthorn Gdns 15 H2
Hawthorne Cres 20 C2
Hawtrey Clo 21 F5
Hawtrey Rd .25 G4
Haymill Rd 10 D4
Haynes Clo 26 A3
Hayse Hill 24 B3
Haywards Mead 19 F6
Hazelhurst Rd 10 C2
Hazell Clo 8 B4
Hazell Way 12 D1
Hazlemere Rd 21 E3
Headington Clo 7 E5
Headington Rd 7 E4
Hearne Dri 16 C5
Heathcote 16 D4
Heathlands Dri 7 E6
Hedingham Mews 7 H5
Helena Rd 25 H4
Helmsdale 7 F3
Helston La 25 E3
Hemson Av 21 F5
Hemwood Rd 24 B5
Hencroft St 20 D5
Hendons Way 16 D5
Henley Rd,
  Burchetts Gdns 6 A2
Henley Rd, Slough 11 E6
Henry Rd 20 B4
Hermitage Clo 21 F5
Hermitage La 25 E5
Heron Dri 26 C3
Herschel St 20 C5
Hetherington Clo 11 E3
Hever Clo 7 G6
Heywood Av 15 E5
Heywood Ct 15 E4
Hibbert Rd 16 C3
High St, Bray 17 E3
High St, Burnham 10 B3
High St, Chalvey 20 A5
High St, Colnbrook 26 D6
High St, Datchet 23 E4
High St, Eton 22 A3
High St, Langley 26 B4
High St, Maidenhead 8 B5
High St, Slough 20 D5
High St, Taplow 9 F3
High St, Windsor 25 H3
High Town Rd 8 A6
Highfield 24 D5
Highfield La 15 E2
Highfield Rd 7 F5
Highgrove Pk 8 A4
Highway Av 7 E5
Highway Rd 7 F6
Hill Farm Rd 9 F2
Hillary Rd 21 H5
Hillersdon 21 E1
Hillmead Ct 9 G4
Hillrise 26 B5
Hillside,
  Maidenhead 15 H1
Hillside, Slough 20 B5
Hilperton Rd 20 C4
Hindhay La 7 F2
Hinksey Clo 26 C2
Hinton Rd 19 E1
Hitcham La 9 F2
Hitcham Rd 9 H3
Hobbis Clo 7 E6
Hockley La 13 E2
Hogarth Clo 19 E1
Hogfair La 10 C3
Hollow Hill La 26 D1
Holly Cres 24 B4
Hollybush Hill 13 E1
Holman Leaze 8 B5
Holmedale 21 F2
Holmlea Rd 23 G5
Holmlea Walk 23 F5
Holmwood Clo 15 F1
Holyport Rd 16 C6
Holyport St 16 C6
Home Farm Way 13 F2
Home Meadow 12 B6
Homers Rd 24 B3
Homestead Rd 15 H2
Homewood 21 G2
Hornbeam Gdns 20 D6
Horseguards Dri 8 D5
Horsemoor Clo 26 B3
Horton Clo 8 D3
Horton Rd,
  Colnbrook 26 C6
Horton Rd,
  Datchet 23 F4
Howard Av 12 B6
Howarth Rd 8 C6
Hubert Rd 21 H6
Hughenden Rd 20 B2
Hull Clo 19 H4
Humber Way 26 B3
Hungerford Av 12 B6
Hungerford Dri 8 A1
Hunter Ct 10 B5
Huntercombe Clo 10 B6

Huntercombe La Nth 10 B5
Huntercombe La Sth 18 B2
Hunts La 9 F2
Hurley La 6 A1
Hurst Rd 10 D5
Hurstfield Dri 10 B6
Hurworth Rd 21 F6
Hylle Clo 24 C3

Ilchester Clo 15 G1
Illingworth 24 C5
Imperial Rd 25 E5
In The Ray 8 D4
India Rd 21 E4

INDUSTRIAL ESTATES:
Bath Rd Retail Pk 11 E6
Canal Ind Est 26 B1
Data Base 15 H2
Foundation Pk 14 D2
Furze Platt Ind Area 7 H2
Heathrow West
  Bus. Park 26 C3
Langley Bus. Centre 26 B1
Maidenhead
  Bus. Campus 14 C4
North Town Ind Est 8 A4
Priors Way Ind Est 16 C4
Progress Bus. Centre 10 C6
Slough Trading Est 11 G6
Vansittart Ind Area 25 F3
Vanwall Bus. Pk 15 G2
Whitebrook Park
  Ind Est 8 D1
Inkerman Rd 19 E5
Institute Rd 9 G5
Iona Cres 10 D6
Ipswich Rd 11 F6
Islett Park Dri 9 E1
Islett Pk 9 E1
Islett Rd 8 D1
Ives Rd 26 B2
Ivy Cres 19 F1

Jacobs Clo 24 C3
James St 25 G3
Jefferson Clo 15 G3
Jellicoe Clo 19 G3
Jennery La 10 C3
John Taylor Ct 20 A4
Journeys End 12 C6
Jubilee Rd 14 A2
Juniper Ct 21 E5
Juniper Dri 8 D5

Kaywood Clo 21 G6
Keats La 8 C6
Keble Rd 7 H5
Kederminster Cotts 26 A1
Keel Dri 19 H3
Keeler Clo 24 C5
Keepers Farm Clo 24 C5
Kelpatrick Rd 10 D6
Kelsey Clo 15 H3
Kendal Clo 20 D3
Kendal Dri 20 D3
Kendrick Rd 21 F6
Kenilworth Clo 20 D6
Kenneally 24 A4
Kennedy Clo 7 G6
Kennett Rd 26 C2
Kennet Rd 8 B5
Kent Av 11 H5
Kent Way 7 H3
Kentons La 24 C4
Kenwood Clo 7 E6
Keppel St 25 H4
Keswick Ct 20 D3
Keys La 8 B6
Kidderminster Rd 11 F2
Kidwells Clo 8 B5
Kiln Pl 7 E1
Kimber Clo 24 D5
Kimberley Clo 26 A3
Kimbers Dri 10 C3
Kimbers La 16 A3
King Edward Ct 25 G3
King Edward St 20 B5
King Edward VII Av 22 B4
King St 8 B6
Kinghorn La 7 H2
Kinghorn Pk 7 H1
Kings Dri 8 A6
Kings Field 24 B3
Kings Gro 8 A6
Kings Rd, Slough 20 B6
Kings Rd, Windsor 25 G6
Kingstable St 22 B4
Kingswood Ct 16 B2
Kinnaird Clo 10 C6
Kirkwall Spur 20 D5
Knights Clo 24 B3
Knolton Way 21 E1
Knowlsey Clo 7 E3
Kola Clo 21 E2

La Roche Clo 21 F5
Laburnham Rd 7 H6
Laburnum Gro 26 C5

Ladbrooke Rd 20 A5
Ladyday Pl 19 H2
Laggan Rd .8 B3
Laggan Sq 8 B3
Lake Av .20 A3
Lake End Ct 10 A6
Lake End Rd 18 A1
Lakeside 8 C3
Lakeside Dri 12 C2
Lambert Av 21 H5
Lambourne Dri 15 G3
Lammas Ct 25 G4
Lammas Rd 10 C4
Lancaster Av 11 H4
Lancaster Rd 7 F4
Lancastria Mews 7 H6
Lancelot Clo 19 G3
Langdale Clo 8 C6
Langley Broom 26 A4
Langley Park Rd 26 B1
Langley Quay 26 B1
Langley Rd,
  Langley 26 A2
Langley Rd,
  Slough 21 F5
Langton Clo 7 G4
Langworthy End 16 D6
Langworthy La 16 C6
Lansdowne Av 20 B4
Lansdowne Ct 20 C4
Lantern Walk 8 D5
Larch Clo 11 H5
Larchfield Rd 15 H2
Larkins La 13 F3
Lascelles Rd 21 E6
Lassell Gdns 8 D5
Laurel Av 21 H5
Lawkland 11 H3
Lawn Cl 23 H4
Lawrence Way 10 C5
Laxton Grn 15 G3
Layburn Cres 26 C5
Leaholme Gdns 10 A5
Ledgers Rd 20 B5
Lee La 6 C2
Leeds Rd 20 B3
Lees Clo 15 F2
Lees Gdns 15 F2
Leeson Gdns 19 E5
Leigh Pk 22 A3
Leigh Rd 19 G1
Leigh Sq 24 B4
Leighton Gdns 8 D4
Leiston Spur 20 B1
Lent Green La 10 B3
Lent Rise Rd 10 A3
Lerwick Dri 20 B1
Lewins Way 19 E1
Lexington Av 15 G1
Liddell 20 A5
Liddell Way 20 A5
Lillibrooke Cres 15 E3
Lime Av 22 D4
Lime Walk 7 E4
Linchfield Rd 23 F5
Lincoln Ct 20 D3
Lincoln Hatch La 10 C4
Lincoln Rd 7 F4
Lincoln Way 18 D1
Linden Av 7 H3
Linden Dri 11 H1
Lindores Rd 10 D6
Lingholm Clo 7 G6
Linkswood Rd 10 B2
Lismore Park 20 C2
Lissett Rd 8 C6
Litcham Spur 20 B2
Little Buntings 26 C4
Little Sutton La 26 C4
Littlebrook Av 10 C3
Littledown Rd 20 C3
Littleport Spur 20 B2
Liverpool Rd 11 G6
Lochinvar Clo 19 G3
Lock Av 8 D2
Lock La 15 G2
Lock Mead 8 D2
Lockbridge Ct 8 D4
Locke Gdns 21 F5
Lockets Clo 24 C3
Loddon Dri 7 H4
Loddon Spur 20 B2
Lodge Clo 19 H3
Lodge Way 24 C5
London Rd,
  Datchet 23 E4
London Rd,
  Langley 26 A3
London Rd,
  Slough 21 E5
Long Dri 10 C3
Long Furlong Dri 11 F4
Long Croft 26 B2
Long Reddings La 11 G4
Longleat Gdns 15 H1
Longmead 24 B3
Longworth Dri 9 E3
Lonsdale Clo 8 C3

Lonsdale Way 16 D5
Loosen Dri 15 E3
Loring Rd 24 D3
Lorne Clo 19 H4
Lorne Ct 19 H4
Losfield Rd 24 C3
Lovejoy La 24 B4
Lovett Gdns 8 D2
Lowbrook Dri 15 E3
Lower Boynton Rd 7 H6
Lower Britwell Rd 10 C4
Lower Cippenham La 19 E2
Lower Cookham Rd 8 D1
Lower Lees Rd 11 G3
Lower Peascod St 25 G3
Lowestoft Dri 10 C6
Ludlow Rd 16 A1
Luff Clo 24 C5
Lutmans La 8 B2
Lydford Av 12 B6
Lydsey Clo 11 F3
Lyell 24 A5
Lynch Hill La 10 D4
Lynden Clo 16 D6
Lyneham Gdns 7 F3
Lynton Grn 7 H5
Lynwood Av 21 G6

Mackenzie Mall 20 C4
Madeira Walk 25 H3
Magnolia Gdns 21 F6
Magpie Way 11 E4
Maidenhead Court Pk 8 D1
Maidenhead Rd,
  Dedworth 24 A2
Maidenhead Rd,
  Datchet 23 F4
Maidenhead Rd,
  Furze Platt 7 H3
Majors Farm Rd 23 G4
Malders La 8 A2
Mallard Dri 19 F1
Mallow Pk 7 G3
Malpas Rd 21 E3
Malton Av 19 G1
Malvern Rd 7 H3
Manor Farm La 24 D5
Manor House La 23 E4
Manor La 16 A2
Manor Rd,
  Maidenhead 16 A2
Manor Rd, Windsor 24 A2
Manor Way 16 C6
Mansel Clo 21 E1
Mansell Clo 24 C4
Mansfield Clo 11 F3
Maple Clo 15 G1
Maple Cres 21 F3
Mapledurham Walk 8 A1
Maplin Park 26 C1
Marbeck Clo 24 B3
Marescroft Rd 11 E4
Marina Way 18 C1
Market La 26 D2
Market St 8 B5
Marlborough Clo 7 E6
Marlborough Rd,
  Maidenhead 7 E6
Marlborough Rd,
  Slough 23 G1
Marlow Rd,
  Furze Platt 6 C1
Marlow Rd,
  Maidenhead 8 A5
Marsh La 17 G1
Marshfield 23 F5
Martin Clo 8 A4
Martin Rd 20 B5
Martins Clo 24 B3
Martins Plain 12 C4
Marunden Grn 11 F3
Maryside 26 A1
Masons Clo 19 E1
Maybury Clo 10 C5
Maypole Rd 10 A5
Mead Av 26 C1
Mead Clo 26 C1
Mead Walk 26 C1
Mead Way 10 C5
Meadfield Av 26 B2
Meadfield Rd 26 B2
Meadow La 25 F1
Meadow Rd 21 H6
Meadow View La 16 A6
Meadow Way 17 G2
Meadway 8 B5
Medallion Pl 8 D5
Medlar Ct 21 F3
Melbourne Av 20 A2
Mendip Clo 26 B4
Mercia Rd 15 F2
Mercian Way 18 D2
Mere Rd 20 D6
Merlin Clo 20 D5
Merton Clo 15 G3
Merton Rd 20 D5
Merwin Way 24 B5
Michael Clo 15 G1
Michaels Path 6 B3
Midcroft 11 G4

Middle Green Rd 21 H3
Middle Walk 10 B3
Middlegreen Rd 21 G5
Mildenhall Rd 20 B2
Mill La,
  Maidenhead 9 E5
Mill La,
  Windsor 25 E2
Mill Pl 23 G5
Mill St 20 D3
Millstream La 19 E2
Milner Rd 12 B5
Milton Rd 12 B5
Milverton Clo 15 F3
Mina Av 21 G5
Minniecroft Rd 10 B3
Minster Way 26 A1
Minton Rise 10 B6
Mirador Cres 21 E2
Missenden Gdns 10 B6
Mitchell Clo 19 G3
Moat Dri 21 F1
Moffey Hill 8 A3
Moneycrower Dri 8 A6
Moneyrow Grn 16 C6
Monkey Island La 17 F3
Monks Rd 24 B4
Monksfield Way 11 F4
Montague Rd,
  Datchet 23 E5
Montague Rd,
  Slough 20 C3
Montem La 20 A4
Montpelier 25 G4
Montrose Av,
  Datchet 23 F4
Montrose Av,
  Slough 11 H5
Montrose Dri 7 E6
Montrose Way 23 G4
Moor End 16 D5
Moor Field Ter 8 C4
Moor La 8 B3
Moorbridge Rd 8 C5
Moore Clo 19 G3
Moores La 19 E5
Moorlands Dri 6 D4
Moorside Clo 8 A3
Moray Dri 21 H2
Moreau Walk 21 H2
Moreland Av 26 D6
Moreland Clo 26 D6
Moreton Way 18 C2
Morley Clo 26 B1
Morrice Clo 26 B3
Mortimer Rd 21 G6
Mossy Vale 7 H3
Mountbatten Clo 20 D5
Mountbatten Sq 25 G3
Muddy La,
  Maidenhead 7 F6
Muddy La, Slough 20 C1
Mulberry Dri 23 H1
Mulberry Walk 7 G4
Mundesley Spur 20 B2
Murrin Rd 7 F5
Myrtle Cres 20 D2

Napier Rd 7 F6
Nash Rd 26 B3
Needham Clo 24 C3
Nelson Clo 23 G1
Nelson Rd 24 D5
Neville Clo 12 C1
New Rd, Datchet 23 G5
New Rd, Holyport 16 D6
New Rd, Langley 26 B4
New Sq 8 B5
Newberry Cres 24 B4
Newberry Way 20 B5
Newbury Dri 8 D6
Newchurch Rd 11 G4
Newhaven Spur 11 G4
Newlands Dri 7 E5
Newnham Clo 20 D4
Newport Rd 10 D4
Newton Clo 26 A1
Nicholls 24 B5
Nicholsons La 8 B5
Nightingale La 7 H1
Nixey Clo 21 E5
Norden Clo 15 G2
Norden Rd 15 G1
Norelands Dri 10 B2
Norfolk Av 11 H5
Norfolk Park Cotts 8 A4
Norfolk Rd 8 A4
Norreys Dri 15 G2
North Burnham Clo 10 B3
North Clo 24 D3
North Dean 8 B4
North Field Rd 8 B3
North Grn,
  Maidenhead 8 B3
North Grn, Slough 20 C3
North Park 26 D2
North Rd 8 A5
North Star La 7 G6

Name	Ref		Name	Ref		Name	Ref		Name	Ref		Name	Ref
North Town Clo	8 B3		Petty Pl	15 H2		Reddington Dri, Slough	21 H6		St Peters Rd	7 H2		Stanhope Rd	10 D6
North Town Mead	8 B4		Pevensey Rd	11 F5		Redford Rd	24 B3		Salisbury Av	11 H4		Stanley Cotts	20 C4
North Town Moor	8 B3		Pheasants Croft	15 E2		Redriff Clo	7 H6		Salisbury Mews	11 H4		Stanley Grn	26 A3
North Town Rd	8 B3		Phipps Clo	15 E4		Redwood Rd	10 A2		Salt Hill Av	19 H2		Stanton Way	23 H1
Northampton Av	20 A1		Phipps Rd	10 D5		Redwood Gdns	20 A2		Salt Hill Dri	20 A3		Starwood Ct	21 F5
Northborough Rd	11 G4		Piece La	11 E1		Reeve Rd	16 D6		Salt Hill Way	20 A3		Station App	8 B6
Northcroft	11 G4		Pierson Rd	24 B3		Reform Rd	8 C5		Salters Clo	8 C5		Station Rd, Burnham	10 D6
Northern Rd	12 A6		Pine Clo	7 F5		Regent Ct, Slough	20 C2		Salters Rd	8 C5		Station Rd, Langley	26 B2
Northfield Rd	19 E5		Pink La	10 A2		Regent Ct, Windsor	25 H3		Sampsons Grn	11 F3		Station Rd, Taplow	9 H5
Northmead Rd	11 E4		Pinkneys Dri	6 C5		Reid Av	15 H1		Sandisplatt Rd	7 E6		Staunton Rd	12 B6
Northumbria Rd	15 F2		Pinkneys Rd	7 E3		Repton Clo	15 G3		Sandlers End	11 G4		Stephenson Dri	25 E2
Norway Dri	21 E1		Pipers Clo	10 B2		Revesby Clo	15 H3		Sandown Rd	11 E5		Stewart Av	20 C1
Nursery La	21 G4		Pitts Rd	19 H2		Ribstone Rd	15 F3		Sandringham Ct	10 D6		Stile Rd	21 G6
Nursery La	10 A6		Plackett Way	18 D2		Richmond Cres	20 D4		Sandringham Rd	8 A2		Stirling Clo	24 B4
			Plough La	13 E3		Rickmans La	12 C1		Sands Farm Dri	10 C4		Stirling Gro	7 E4
Oak La	25 E3		Plough Lees La	20 C3		Ridgebank	19 F1		Sandy Mead	16 D5		Stirling Rd	11 F5
Oak Stubbs La	17 G2		Plymouth Rd	11 E5		Riding Court Rd	23 F4		Sawyers Clo	24 C2		Stockdales Rd	19 E5
Oaken Gro	7 F4		Pococks La	22 B2		Ripley Clo	26 A2		Sawyers Cres	15 E4		Stockwells	9 F3
Oakfield Av	19 G2		Pool La	20 B3		Risborough Rd	8 A4		Saxon Clo	26 A1		Stoke Court Dri	12 C3
Oakhurst	8 D1		Poolmans Rd	24 B5		Riseley Rd	7 G6		Saxon Gdns	9 F4		Stoke Gdns	20 C3
Oakley Cres	20 B2		Popes Clo	26 C6		River Gdns	17 E2		Scafell Rd	11 E4		Stoke Grn	12 D5
Oakley Green Rd	24 A3		Poplars Gro	8 D2		River Rd	9 E6		Scarborough Way	19 G3		Stoke Park Av	11 H3
Oatlands Dri	20 A1		Portland Clo	10 C4		River St	25 G2		School La, Maidenhead	8 A3		Stoke Poges La, Slough	20 B4
Ockwells Rd	11 F3		Portlock Rd	7 G5		Riverside Walk	25 H2		School La, Wexham St	13 E2		Stoke Poges La, Stoke Grn	12 C6
Odencroft Rd	11 F3		Portsmouth Ct	20 C2		Rixman Clo	7 H5		Seacourt Rd	26 C2		Stoke Rd	20 C4
Old Court Clo	15 F3		Post Office La	15 F2		Rixon Clo	21 H1		Second Cres	20 A1		Stokesay	20 D2
Old Fives Ct	10 B3		Powis Clo	15 F2		Roasthill La	18 C6		Sefton Clo	12 D2		Stomp Rd	10 B5
Old Forge Clo	16 C3		Powney Rd	7 G5		Robin Hood Clo	19 E2		Sefton Paddock	13 E1		Stompits Rd	16 D6
Old Marsh La	17 G2		Poyle La	10 A1		Rochford Way	9 H6		Sermed Ct	21 F3		Stonebridge Field	19 H6
Old Mill La	17 E2		Preston Rd	21 F3		Rochfords Gdns	21 F3		Severn Cres	26 C4		Stonefield Pk	7 G5
Oldacres	8 D5		Prestwood	21 E2		Roebuck Grn	18 D2		Seymour Clo	15 F3		Stoney La	11 G1
Oldershaw Ms	7 F4		Prince Alberts Walk	23 E5		Rogers La	12 D2		Seymour Rd	20 A4		Stoney Meade	19 G2
Oldfield Rd	8 C6		Prince Andrews Clo	8 C4		Rokesby Rd	11 E2		Shackleton Rd	20 C3		Stour Clo	19 G4
Oldway La	18 D3		Prince Andrews Rd	8 C4		Romsey Clo	26 B2		Shaggy Calf La	20 D2		Stovell Rd	25 F2
Oldways La	18 C2		Prince Consort Cotts	25 G4		Ronaldsay Spur	20 B1		Sharney Av	26 C2		Stowe Rd	19 E1
Opal Ct	13 F6		Princes Clo	19 E6		Roseleigh Clo	7 F3		Sheehy Way	25 F2		Stranraer Gdns	20 C4
Opendale Rd	10 B5		Princes Av	21 E4		Roses La	24 C4		Sheepcote Rd, Eton Wick	19 F6		Stratfield Rd	20 D4
Orchard Av, Burnham	10 C5		Princess St	25 F5		Rosken Gro	11 G2		Sheepcote Rd, Windsor	24 C4		Stratford Clo	10 D4
Orchard Av, Windsor	25 E3		Priors Clo	16 D4		Ross Rd	15 H2		Sheephouse Rd	8 D3		Stratford Gdns	15 G3
Orchard Clo	16 C3		Priors Clo, Slough	20 D5		Rossiter Clo	21 H6		Sheet St	25 H4		Stroma Ct	18 D1
Orchard Gro	7 G5		Priors Rd	24 B5		Rowland Clo	24 B5		Sheffield Rd	20 A2		Stroud Clo	24 B5
Orchardville	10 B4		Priors Way	16 D4		Rowley La	13 F2		Shelley Clo	26 B4		Stroud Farm Rd	16 D6
Orwell Clo	25 G5		Priory Rd	10 B5		Roxborough Way	14 D2		Shenstone Dri	10 C4		Stuart Clo	24 D4
Osborne Ct	25 G4		Priory Way	23 E4		Roxwell Clo	19 E2		Sherbourne Dri, Maidenhead	15 G3		Stuart Way	24 C4
Osborne Ms	25 G4		Providence Pl	8 B5		Royston Way	10 C5		Sherbourne Dri, Windsor	24 D6		Sturt Grn	16 A6
Osborne Rd	25 G4		Purssell Clo	15 E3		Ruby Clo	19 G4		Sherman Rd	20 C1		Suffolk Clo	10 D6
Osborne St	20 C5		Purton La	12 A2		Ruddlesway	24 B3		Sherwood Clo	21 H6		Suffolk Rd	15 H2
Osney Rd	8 A2					Ruscombe Gdns	23 E3		Sherwood Dri	7 E6		Sumburgh Spur	20 B1
Ostlergate	7 G3		Quantock Clo	26 B4		Rushington Av	16 B1		Shifford Cres	8 A2		Summerlea	19 G2
Oxford Av, Burnham	10 A2		Quaves Rd	21 F5		Russel St	25 G4		Shirley Av	24 D3		Summerleaze Rd	8 C3
Oxford Av, Slough	11 E5		Queen Annes Rd	25 G6		Russell Ct	8 B5		Shirley Rd	15 G1		Summers Rd	10 B3
Oxford Rd	25 F3		Queen Elizabeths Walk	22 C5		Russet Rd	15 G3		Shoppenhangers Rd	16 A2		Sun Clo	22 A3
Oxford St	25 G3		Queen St	20 C4		Rutherford Clo	24 D3		Shoreham Rise	10 C4		Sun La	8 A5
			Queen Victorias Walk	22 C4		Rutland Av	20 A1		Shortfern	21 F2		Sunbury Rd	22 B3
Padstow Clo	26 A1		Queens Acre	25 G6		Rutland Gate	7 G6		Sidney Rd	24 A6		Sunderland Rd	7 F4
Paget Dri	15 E2		Queens Ct	20 D3		Rutland Pl	7 G6		Silco Dri	8 A6		Surly Hall Clo	24 D3
Paget Rd	26 A3		Queens Mead	23 E4		Rutland Rd	7 G6		Silver Clo	15 E1		Surrey Av	11 H4
Palmers Clo	15 E4		Queens Rd, Datchet	23 E4		Rydings	24 C5		Silvertrees Dri	15 E1		Sussex Clo	21 E5
Palmerston Av	21 F5		Queens Rd, Eton Wick	19 E6		Rye Clo	15 E2		Simmons Clo	26 B3		Sussex Pl	21 E5
Pantile Row	25 H4		Queens Rd, Slough	20 C3		Ryecroft	24 D5		Simpson Clo	8 C4		Sutton Av	21 F5
Park Clo	25 H4		Queens Rd, Windsor	25 G4		Rylstone Clo	15 G3		Slough Rd, Datchet	22 D1		Sutton Clo	15 D1
Park Corner	24 C5		Queensmere Rd	20 D4		Ryvers Rd	26 A2		Slough Rd, Eton	22 B2		Sutton La	26 C5
Park Gate	10 C4		Queensway	8 A2					Smithfield Rd	15 E3		Sutton Pl	26 C5
Park La	21 E6		Quinbrookes	21 F2		Sadlers Ms	8 D5		Smiths La	24 C4		Swabey Rd	26 B3
Park Rd	12 A4					Saffron Clo	23 F5		Snape Spur	20 B1		Switchback Clo	7 H2
Park St, Maidenhead	8 B5		Radcot Av	26 C2		St Adrians Clo	15 F2		Snowball Hill	15 F6		Switchback Rd	7 H1
Park St, Slough	20 D5		Radcot Clo	8 A2		St Albans St	25 H4		Snowdon Clo	24 B6		Switchback Rd Nth	7 H2
Park St, Windsor	25 H3		Radnor Way	23 H1		St Andrews Av	24 D4		Somerford Ct	8 D4		Switchback Rd Sth	7 H2
Parkland Av	23 G1		Ragstone Rd	20 B5		St Andrews Cres	24 D5		Somersby Cres	15 H3		Sycamore Clo	15 F3
Parkside	7 H3		Railway Ter	20 C4		St Andrews Way	18 D1		Somerville Rd	19 H6		Sycamore Walk	21 H2
Parkside Walk	20 D6		Raleigh Clo	19 F2		St Bernards Rd	21 F6		Sospel Ct	11 H2		Sydney Gro	20 A2
Parkview Chase	10 D6		Rambler Clo	10 B6		St Chads Rd	15 F2		South Clo	18 C1		Sykes Rd	11 G5
Parlaunt Rd	26 B3		Rambler La	21 G6		St Cloud Way	8 B5		South Field Clo	18 C4		Sylvester Rd	8 A2
Parry Grn	26 B3		Ramsey Ct	10 C4		St Columbus Clo	15 F2		South Grn	20 C3		
Parsonage La, Slough	12 A4		Randall Clo	26 A3		St Elmo Clo	12 A6		South Meadow La	25 G2		Tachbrook Clo	8 B4
Parsonage La, Windsor	25 E3		Randolph Rd	21 H6		St Elmo Cres	12 A6		South Rd	8 A6		Talbot Av	26 A1
Partridge Mead	8 B2		Ravensfield	21 G4		St Georges Clo	24 C3		Southcroft	11 G4		Talbot Rd	23 G5
Patricia Clo	18 D1		Ravensworth Rd	11 F3		St Georges Cres	18 C1		Southfield Gdns	10 B5		Talbots Dri	7 E6
Paxton Av	19 H4		Ray Dri	8 D5		St Ives Rd	8 B5		Southlea Rd	23 E5		Tamar Way	26 C3
Pearce Clo	8 B3		Ray Lea Clo	8 C4		St James Rd	10 B6		Southwold Spur	26 D1		Tamarisk Way	19 G2
Pearce Rd	8 B3		Ray Lea Rd	8 C3		St Johns Dri	25 E4		Spackmans Way	20 A6		Tangier Ct	22 B3
Pearl Gdns	19 G2		Ray Mead Clo	8 D3		St Johns Rd, Slough	20 D2		Spencer Rd	26 A2		Tangier La	22 B3
Peascod St	25 G3		Ray Mead Rd	8 D5		St Johns Rd, Windsor	25 E4		Spencers Clo	7 G4		Taplow Common Rd	10 A1
Peel Clo	25 E5		Ray Mill Rd	8 C3		St Laurence Way	20 D5		Spencers Rd	7 G5		Taplow Rd	10 A5
Peel Ct	11 H5		Ray Mill Rd E	8 C3		St Leonards Av	24 C5		Sperling Rd	8 B3		Tarbay La	24 A4
Pemberton Rd	11 E4		Ray Mill Rd W	8 B4		St Leonards Hill	24 C5		Spinners Walk	25 G3		Tavistock Clo	7 E5
Penn Meadow	12 D3		Ray Park Av	8 D3		St Leonards Rd	25 G4		Spinney	19 G2		Taylors Ct	7 F4
Penn Rd, Datchet	23 G5		Ray Park La	8 C5		St Lukes Rd	8 A5		Spring Clo	8 B2		Teesdale Rd	11 F5
Penn Rd, Slough	12 A6		Ray Park Rd	8 C5		St Margarets Rd	7 E5		Spring Hill	16 A3		Telford Dri	19 G2
Pennine Rd	11 F5		Ray St	8 C5		St Marks Cres	7 F5		Spring La	19 F2		Temple Rd	25 G4
Pennylets Grn	12 D1		Raymond Rd, Maidenhead	7 H5		St Marks Rd	25 G4		Springate Field	21 H5		Tennyson Way	10 D4
Penshurst Rd	15 G1		Raymond Rd, Slough	26 B2		St Marks Rd, Maidenhead	7 G5		Springfield Pk	16 D5		Testwood Rd	24 B3
Pentland Rd	11 F5		Rayners Clo	26 D6		St Marks Rd, Windsor	25 G4		Springfield Rd, Slough	26 C5		Thames Av	25 H2
Penyston Rd	7 G6		Rays Av	24 D2		St Marys Rd, Langley	26 A1		Springfield Rd, Windsor	25 E4		Thames Cres	8 D2
Penzance Spur	11 G4		Rectory Clo, Slough	11 H2		St Marys Rd, Slough	21 H4		Stafferton Way	8 B6		Thames Mead	24 C3
Pepys Clo	26 C5		Rectory Clo, Windsor	25 E3		St Michaels Ct	10 C4		Stafford Av	11 H4		Thames Rd	26 C3
Percy Pl	23 F4		Rectory Rd	9 F3		St Patricks Clo	15 F2		Stafford Clo	10 B6		Thames St	25 H2
Perrycroft	24 C5		Red Cottage Ms	21 F6		St Pauls Av	20 D3		Stamford Rd	15 G1		Thameside	25 H2
Perryfields Way	10 B4		Red Ct	20 B4		St Peters Clo	10 B4					Thatchers Dri	15 E1
Perryman Way	11 E3		Reddington Dri, Langley	26 A3								The Avenue, Datchet	23 E5
Perth Av	11 G6											The Avenue, Maidenhead	8 D2
Peterhead Mews	26 B4												
Petersfield Av	20 D3												

The Binghams	16 C3	
The Briars	26 A4	
The Cherries	21 F2	
The Close	18 C1	
The Courtyards	26 B1	
The Crescent, Maidenhead	8 A5	
The Crescent, Slough	20 B5	
The Croft	15 G1	
The Dell	15 E4	
The Drive, Datchet	23 F5	
The Drive, Slough	21 H5	
The Fairway, Burnham	10 C3	
The Fairway, Maidenhead	15 F3	
The Farthingales	8 D5	
The Frithe	21 E2	
The Glen	21 G6	
The Gore	9 H2	
The Green, Burnham	10 B4	
The Green, Datchet	23 E4	
The Green, Slough	20 A5	
The Greenway	18 D2	
The Grove	20 D5	
The Hatch	24 A2	
The Link	21 F2	
The Long Walk	25 H5	
The Mews	20 C6	
The Myrke	22 D1	
The Normans	21 E1	
The Paddock, Datchet	23 E5	
The Paddock, Maidenhead	7 G3	
The Pagoda	8 D3	
The Parade	24 B3	
The Points	15 F3	
The Pound	10 C4	
The Precincts	10 B4	
The Redwoods	25 G5	
The Ridings	7 E6	
The Rushes	8 D6	
The Spur	10 D5	
The Terrace	17 E3	
The Walk	19 F6	
The Went	26 D6	
The Wheatbutts	19 F5	
The Wicketts	7 G5	
Thicket Gro	6 D5	
Third Cres	20 A1	
Thirkelby Clo	19 H2	
Thirlmere Av	10 B5	
Thompson Clo	26 B3	
Thorn Dri	21 H1	
Thorndike	11 G4	
Thrift La	15 G4	
Thurlby Way	15 H3	
Thurston Rd	20 B1	
Tilstone Av	19 E6	
Tilstone Clo	19 E5	
Timbers Walk	15 F1	
Tinkers La	24 B4	
Tintern Clo	19 H4	
Tithe Barn Dri	17 F5	
Tithe Clo	16 D5	
Tithe Ct	26 B3	
Tockley Rd	10 B3	
Tollgate	7 E6	
Tomlin Rd	11 E4	
Topaz Clo	19 H2	
Torquay Spur	11 G3	
Torridge Rd	26 C5	
Travic Rd	11 F3	
Travis Ct	11 G2	
Treesmill Dri	15 G3	
Trelawney Av, Langley	26 A2	
Trelawney Av, Slough	21 G6	
Trenchard Rd	16 D6	
Trent Rd	26 C5	
Trinity Pl	25 G4	
Troutbeck Clo	20 D3	
Truro Clo	7 E5	
Tubwell Rd	13 F3	
Tudor Ct	8 D1	
Tudor Gdns	10 C5	
Tudor Way	24 C3	
Tunis La	20 A4	
Turner Rd	21 F5	
Turnoak Pk	24 C5	
Turpins Grn	15 E1	
Turton Way	20 B5	
Tweed Rd	26 C5	
Twinches La	19 G2	
Twynham Rd	7 F5	
Tyrrell Gdns	24 D5	
Ullswater Clo	10 C5	
Umberville Way	11 E3	
Underhill Clo	7 H6	
Upcroft	25 E5	
Upper Bray Rd	16 D4	
Upper Lees Rd	11 G3	
Upton Clo	20 D6	
Upton Court Rd	20 D6	
Upton Pk	20 C5	
Upton Rd	20 D6	
Uxbridge Rd	21 E5	
Vale Gro	20 C6	
Vale Rd	24 D2	
Vansittart Rd	25 F3	
Vantage Rd	19 G2	
Vanwall Rd	15 G2	
Vaughan Gdns	19 E5	
Vermont Rd	11 E4	
Verney Rd	26 B2	
Vicarage Dri	16 D2	
Vicarage Pl	21 E5	
Vicarage Rd	8 A4	
Vicarage Walk	16 D2	
Vicarage Way	26 D6	
Victor Clo	7 F4	
Victor Rd	25 G5	
Victoria Rd, Eton Wick	19 E5	
Victoria Rd, Slough	20 C5	
Victoria St, Slough	20 C5	
Victoria St, Windsor	25 G3	
Village Rd	18 B4	
Villiers Rd	12 A6	
Wade Dri	19 F2	
Wakefield Cres	12 C1	
Waldeck Rd	8 C5	
Wallis Ct	21 E5	
Walker Rd	16 B2	
Walpole Rd	10 C6	
Waltham Clo	14 D4	
Waltham Rd	14 D6	
Walton La	11 E2	
Ward Gdns	19 E1	
Warner Clo	16 D2	
Warren Clo	21 H6	
Warrington Av	20 A1	
Warwick Av	11 H4	
Warwick Clo	15 F3	
Washington Dri, Cippenham	18 D1	
Washington Dri, Windsor	24 C5	
Waterbeach Rd	20 A1	
Waterside Dri	26 B1	
Wavell Clo	11 F3	
Wavell Rd	7 F6	
Waverley Rd	20 A1	
Wayside Ms	8 B4	
Webb Clo	21 H6	
Webster Clo	15 E1	
Webster Ct	7 G6	
Weekes Dri	19 G2	
Welbeck Rd	15 G1	
Welby Clo	15 E2	
Welden	21 F1	
Welland Clo	26 C4	
Wellbank	9 F3	
Wellcroft Rd	19 H2	
Wellesley Rd	20 D4	
Wellhouse Rd	8 A2	
Wellington Rd	7 H5	
Wellington St	20 C4	
Wells Clo	25 E3	
Wendover Rd	10 B5	
Wentworth Av	11 F2	
Wentworth Cres	7 G6	
Wessex Way	15 F2	
West Cres	24 D3	
West Dean	8 B4	
West End Ct	12 D2	
West End La	12 C3	
West Point	18 C2	
West Rd	8 A6	
West St	8 B5	
Westacott Way	14 B1	
Westborough Rd	7 G6	
Westbrook	17 F5	
Westcroft	11 G4	
Westfield La	21 H2	
Westfield Rd, Maidenhead	7 F6	
Westfield Rd, Slough	11 H4	
Westgate Cres	19 F1	
Westlands Av	10 C6	
Westlands Clo	10 C6	
Westmead, Maidenhead	8 B2	
Westmead, Windsor	25 F5	
Westmorland Rd	7 H6	
Weston Rd	11 E5	
Wethered Dri	10 B5	
Wexham Park La	13 F6	
Wexham Rd	13 E6	
Wexham Woods	13 F6	
Wheatfield Clo	15 E2	
Wheatland Rd	21 F6	
Whitby Rd	20 A2	
Whitchurch Clo	8 A2	
White Clo	20 B3	
White Hart Rd, Maidenhead	8 B5	
White Hart Rd, Slough	20 A6	
White Horse Rd	24 B5	
White Paddock	15 E4	
White Rock	8 C3	
Whiteford Rd	12 C6	
Whitehaven	20 D3	
Whiteley	24 C2	
Whites La	23 E3	
Whittaker Rd	10 D4	
Whittenham Clo	20 D3	
Whurley Way	8 A2	
Widbrook Rd	8 D1	
Wildgreen	26 B3	
Wilford Rd	26 A2	
Willant Clo	14 D4	
William St	20 C4	
William St	20 C4	
Willowers	11 G4	
Willoughby Rd	26 B2	
Winbury Ct	8 A6	
Winchester Dri	15 F3	
Windermere Way	10 B5	
Windmill Clo	25 F4	
Windmill Rd	20 A4	
Windrush Av	26 C2	
Windrush Way	8 B4	
Windsor Clo	10 C4	
Windsor La	10 C4	
Windsor Rd, Bray	16 C3	
Windsor Rd, Datchet	22 D3	
Windsor Rd, Slough	20 C6	
Winkfield Rd	24 D6	
Winter Hill Rd	7 E2	
Winvale	20 C6	
Winwood	21 F2	
Withy Croft	21 H2	
Witney Rd	24 C3	
Wolf La	24 B5	
Wood Clo	25 G6	
Wood La	19 F3	
Woodcote	7 H6	
Woodfield Dri	15 E1	
Woodford Way	11 F3	
Woodhurst Rd	8 D3	
Woodland Av, Slough	20 B3	
Woodland Av, Windsor	24 D6	
Woodlands Park Av	15 E4	
Woodlands Park Rd	15 E4	
Woodstock Av	23 G1	
Woodstock Clo	8 B3	
Wootton Way	15 G1	
Worcester Clo	15 G3	
Worcester Gdns	20 B5	
Wordsworth Rd	10 D4	
Wren Ct	26 B2	
Wright	24 B5	
Wyatt Clo	24 B5	
Wylands Rd	26 B3	
Wymers Clo	10 D4	
Wymers Wood Rd	10 A1	
Wyndham Cres	10 B2	
Yarmouth Rd	11 H6	
Ye Meads	17 G4	
Yeovil Rd	11 E5	
Yew Tree Clo	8 A5	
Yew Tree Rd	20 D6	
York Av, Slough	20 A4	
York Av, Windsor	25 F4	
York Rd, Maidenhead	8 B6	
York Rd, Windsor	25 F4	

COOKHAM

Alleyns La	4 D1
Barnfield Clo	4 E4
Bass Mead	4 E4
Bedwins La	4 B3
Bigfrith La	4 A3
Bradcutts La	4 D1
Briar Glen	4 E3
Bridge Av	4 E4
Broom Hill	4 D3
Burnt Oak	4 E2
Cannondown Rd	4 E4
Cedar Dri	4 F3
Choke La	4 A6
Church Rd	4 B3
Cookham Dean Bottom	4 B2
Coombe End	4 A3
Coxborrow Clo	4 E3
Danes Gdns	4 F3
Deans La	4 B1
Elizabeth Clo	4 F2
Gainsborough	4 E4
Gorse Rd	4 D3
Graham Rd	4 E3
Grange La	4 E1
Grange Rd	4 E2
Groves Way	4 E2
Grubwood La	4 A3
Halldore Rd	4 D2
Hardings Grn	4 C2
High Rd	4 D2
Hillcrest Av	4 C2
Hills La	4 C2
Hockett La	4 A3
Hollybush La	4 A3
Inwood Clo	4 C2
Jobs La	4 A3
Kings La	4 B2
Lesters Rd	4 D3
Lightlands La	4 E4
Long La	4 B4
Lower Rd	4 D2
Lyndhurst Av	4 E3
Maidenhead Rd	4 E4
New Rd	4 E3
Peace La	4 E3
Penling Clo	4 B3
Popes La	4 C4
Poundfield La	4 F2
Quarry Wood Rd	4 A1
Riverwood Av	4 A1
Riverwood Dri	4 A1
Roman Lea	4 F2
Rose Bank Clo	4 E2
School La	4 B3
South Wood Gdns	4 C4
Southwood Rd	4 E4
Spencers La	4 D3
Spring La	4 B1
Startins La	4 B1
Station Hill	4 F2
Station Rd	4 F2
Strand La	4 E4
Stubbles La	4 A3
Switchback Rd	4 D4
Terrys La	4 E1
The Shaw	4 D4
Vivien Clo	4 E3
Wakelins End	4 E2
Warners Hill	4 C2
Wessons Hill	4 B2
Westwood Grn	4 F3
Whyteladyes La	4 D2
Windmill Rd	4 B1
Winter Hill	4 B1
Worster Rd	4 E3

FARNHAM COMMON

Andrew Hill La	5 C1
Ashenden Walk	5 C3
Badgers Wood	5 C4
Barn Clo	5 B3
Beaconsfield Rd	5 B3
Bedford Dri	5 B4
Beeches La	5 B3
Beeches Rd	5 B4
Blackpond La	5 B5
Bracken Clo	5 C3
Cages Wood Dri	5 B6
Cherry Tree Rd	5 B6
Christmas La	5 B2
Clare Dri	5 B1
Collinswood Rd	5 A1
Collum Green Rd	5 D2
Common Wood	5 C3
Coppice Way	5 C1
Cottage Park Rd	5 D1
Crispin Way	5 C3
Crown La	5 A6
Dell Clo	5 B4
Drew Meadow	5 B3
Dukes Dri	5 A3
Egypt La	5 A1
Elkins Rd	5 D1
Elm Clo	5 B5
Farnham Park La	5 B6
Forge Dri	5 B5
Foxhollow Dri	5 C4
Frensham Walk	5 B4
Gold Oak La	5 B5
Grange Gdns	5 C4
Green La	5 B5
Gregory Rd	5 C1
Gypsy La	5 D3
Hammond End	5 D3
Hawthorn Dri	5 A6
Heatherside Gdns	5 C2
Hedgerley Hill	5 D1
Hill Pl	5 B6
Holly Clo	5 B5
Ingleglen	5 B4
Jones Way	5 D1
Kennedy Clo	5 B5
Kingsway	5 B5
Langtons Meadow	5 B5
Linden Dri	5 B6
Long Clo	5 B6
Longfield	5 D1
Lord Mayors Dri	5 A4
Mayflower Way	5 C4
Mount Clo	5 C3
One Pin La	5 C2
Orchard Gate	5 B4
Parish La	5 B1
Parsonage La	5 C5
Purton Ct	5 B6
Purton La	5 C6
Reade Ct	5 B5
Robert Rd	5 C1
Romsey Dri	5 B4
Rosewood Way	5 B4
Rowanhurst Dri	5 C4
Scotlands Dri	5 B5
Scott Clo	5 B4
Sherbourne Walk	5 C3
Sir Henry Peeks Dri	5 A5
Spring La	5 B5
Stevenson Rd	5 D1
Stewarts Dri	5 B4
Temple Way	5 C4
Templewood La	5 B4
The Avenue	5 B3
Thompkins La	5 A6
Victoria Rd	5 B5
Wood End Clo	5 C2
Woodland Glade	5 C2

OLD WINDSOR

Albany Rd	27 A3
Albert Rd	27 A2
Ashbrook Rd	27 B5
Aylesworth Spur	27 B5
Burfield Rd	27 A4
Cell Farm Av	27 B3
Church Rd	27 B3
Clayhall La	27 A3
Coppice Dri	27 D5
Cornwall Rd	27 A4
Crimp Hill	27 A4
Crimp Hill Rd	27 A3
Datchet Rd	27 A2
Fairfield App	27 B4
Fairfield Rd	27 D4
Farm Dri	27 C4
Follet Clo	27 B4
Friary Rd	27 B4
Garson La	27 D5
Glebe Rd	27 B3
Gregory Dri	27 B4
Grove Clo	27 C5
Hartley Copse	27 A4
Harwood Gdns	27 B5
Keppel Spur	27 B5
King Johns Clo	27 C4
Kingsbury Dri	27 B3
Kingswood Creek	27 D3
Lyndwood Dri	27 A4
Magna Carta La	27 D6
Malt House Clo	27 C5
Meadow Clo	27 B4
Meadow Way	27 B4
Millers La	27 A4
Mills Spur	27 B5
Newton Ct	27 B4
Newton La	27 B4
Nursery Way	27 D4
Old Ferry Dri	27 B4
Orchard Rd	27 B4
Ouseley Rd	27 C5
Park Av	27 D3
Pelling Hill	27 B5
Pollards Clo	27 B3
Priest Hill	27 C6
Queens Clo	27 B3
Ricardo Rd	27 C5
Riverside	27 C5
Robin Willis Way	27 A4
St Andrews Clo	27 A4
St Lukes Rd	27 B3
St Peters Clo	27 B3
Saxon Way	27 A2
Southlea Rd	27 C5
Straight Rd	27 B3
The Avenue	27 A4
The Crofters	27 A4
The Drive	27 D3
The Embankment	27 D5
The Friary	27 C4
The Grange	27 C5
Tudor La	27 C5
Tyle Pl	27 A3
Walpole Rd	27 B5
Warrington Spur	27 B5
Wharf Rd	27 C5
William Ellis Clo	27 A3
Windsor Rd	27 C6